Monitions of a Mountain Man

Manna, Money, and Me

Copyright © 2009
by
David E. Robinson

All Rights Reserved
Parts of this book may be reproduced subject to due and specific acknowledgment of their source.

Maine-Patriot.com
3 Linnell Circle
Brunswick, Maine 04011

maine-patriot.com

"...the trumpet that shall never call retreat..."

*If we are ignorant of evil's nature
we are not protected from its harmful influence*

*"A knowledge of error and of its operations must
precede that understanding of Truth which destroys
error"*

Monitions of a Mountain Man
Contents

Foreword -- 9
Introduction -- 11
1. The Pillage Of America ------------------------- 13
2. The Power To Coin Money ---------------------- 21
3. The Costs Of The National Debt ---------------- 29
4. Sound And Stable Money ----------------------- 37
5. What Famous Men Have Said -------------------- 45
6. How Things Came To Be ------------------------ 53
7. How things Are Now ---------------------------- 87
8. Money? Or Mammon?-------------------------- 113
9. America? A Conquered Land? ------------------ 117
10. Restoring America ------------------------------ 125
11. It's Time For The Solution --------------------- 129
12. Abolish The Federal Reserve ------------------- 137
13. Emergency Powers Act Of 1933 ---------------- 141

APPENDIX

Executive Order Farce ------------------------- 155
Powers And Duties Of Congress -------------- 157
Treason In Congress --------------------------- 161
Panama Giveaway ------------------------------ 175
Opposition To The U.N. ----------------------- 183
The Main Purpose Of The 2nd Amendment -- 185
Epilogue -- 189

Foreword

The Mountain Man is a Codger who lived in a small farming community, in a high mountain valley at the base of *The Roan* — one of the two highest mountain peaks on the eastern seaboard, on the North Carolina/Tennessee State line. The *Roan* is but a few feet lower than *Mount Mitchell*, just off the Blue Ridge Parkway, midway between Asheville and Boone.

Mitchell County is bordered on the North by the Appalachian Trail that runs all the way from Maine down to Georgia, and on the South by the *Blue Ridge Parkway* that runs all the way from Washington, D.C. down the *Blue Ridge* to Cherokee, North Carolina — and on the East and West by branches of the *Toe River*, a wild river flowing down *the Gorge* into Tennessee.

In another of his books The Mountain Man writes:

Civilization must be acquired anew by every upcoming generation. Any serious interruption in its *transmission* or its *financing* may bring it to an ignoble end.

Mortal man differs from the beast only by *education* — by the *spiritualization of thought.*

Print, commerce, and a thousand other ways of communication bind civilizations to one another. They preserve for future cultures all that is of value to their own. Let us then, *as we pass along this way,* gather up and save our heritage, and offer it to our children, in **witness to the truth.**

I will lift mine eyes unto the hills, from whence cometh my help. My help cometh from the Lord. — Psalm 121:1

Prologue

Few prople now feel and live as people lived when our nation began, when our forefathers' prayers blended with the murmuring winds of their forest home. We live in a period of doubts, inquiry, speculation, selfishness, of divided interests, marvelous good, and mysterious evil. But sin can only destroy itself, and reform must push on the growth of mankind.

Honor bestowed on faithful merit is delayed, as it always has been, but is sure to follow.

The reformer has little time to give in his own defense. No sacrifice is too great for the quiet endurance of this loving care.

What has not unselfed love achieved for the race? All that was ever accomplished, and more than history has recorded.

The reformer works on, unmentioned save when he is abused or his work is questioned or maligned. He labors for the establishment of a cause which is fraught with infinite blessings. But what of all that? Who should care for *everybody?*

Yet the good *done* and the love that foresees *more* to do, are an ever-present reward. Let one's life *answer well* these questions and it *already* hath a benediction: **Well done good and faithful servant.**

"*Who is telling mankind of the foe in ambush? Is the informer one who seen the foe? If so, listen and be wise. Escape from evil, and designate those as unfaithful stewards who have seen the danger and yet have given no warning."* — Mary Baker Eddy.

Chapter 1
The Pillage Of America

WE LIVE IN A SOCIETY GOVERNED BY MONEY
Fiscally educated money men know that the great money powers of the world are centered around the world's Central Banks — *like the Bank of England and the Federal Reserve Bank of the United States,* — and that these Central Banks secretly rule the governments of the world while allowing the *illusion* of "Democracy" to exist in the minds of the people.

The influence of money is so pervasive that most people never give it a second thought even though it virtually controls their lives. But rather than worshiping before the alter of the money god — *Mammon* — far better it is to worship the true source of all life, the all-loving Creator of the Universe and all that therein is.

In truth, though vain men — *who would rule the world through their great deceptions* — may have temporary success, they will ultimately learn that God is the "all seeing Eye" — the Source of all true thought — the One true ruler of the world; and let the love, mercy, and light of God shine forth on the human scene!

THE CREATION OF MONEY
"If the American people ever allow private banks to control the issue of their money, first by inflation and then by deflation, the banks and corporations that will grow up around them (around the banks), will deprive the people of their property until their children will wake up homeless on the continent their fathers conquered." — Thomas Jefferson.

Today money is generally "created" by central Banks, such as the Bank of England or the Federal Reserve Bank of the United States. The Constitution of the United States says that Congress is to mint the money and set the value thereof for the United States. But in 1913, the Federal Reserve Act was passed by intentional mistake. This Act simply **gave** Congress' constitutional authority to create money to the *private* Cabal of Banks called collectively the Federal Reserve Bank. Even though the Federal Reserve Bank is secretive about who it's owning banks or shareholders are, it is *now* known that the "class A" stocks in the Federal Reserve Bank are held by the following eight family institutions:

1. Rothschild Banks of London and Berlin.
2. Lazard Brothers Bank of Paris.
3. Israel Moses Seif Bank of Italy.
4. Warburg Bank of Hamburg and Amsterdam.
5. Lehman Bank of New York.
6. Kuhn Loeb Bank of N.Y.
7. Chase Manhattan Bank of N.Y.
8. Goldman Sachs Bank of N.Y.

The *remaining* stock is held by the Chemical Trust and the Rockefeller Trust. These stockholders hold United States Federal Government Bonds which amount to more than $9.5 Trillion dollars, and growing, — otherwise known today as the United States "National Debt!" (Federal Debt.) These *private* stockholders' annual profits from interest payments alone are hundreds of Billion dollars per year!

Before the passage of the Federal Reserve Act, Congress could print its own treasury notes — its own money — and use this money to pay for the cost of the U.S. Government. Ever since the passage of the Federal Reserve Act in 1913, Congress has had to **borrow** all of its money from the privately owned non-federal Federal Reserve Bank *at interest!* Furthermore, the Federal Reserve Act is unconstitutional and therefore against the Constitutional laws of the land! Even though the Chairman of the Federal Reserve Marketing Board is appointed by the President of the United States, the so-called *"Federal"* Reserve Bank is *not* any part of the United States Government, no moreso than Federal Express!

There have been numerous attempts by Congress to pass legislation to have the General Accounting Office (GAO) audit the Federal Reserve Bank. But all such attempts thus far have failed, — primarily because Congress cannot force an audit on a private company. However, the Federal Reserve Bank can order the U.S. Treasury to print a determined amount of Federal Reserve Notes and have the U.S. Mint deliver them to the Federal Reserve Bank for merely the cost of printing, — a small fraction of the face value of the notes. These paper Federal Reserve Notes are then *loaned* into circulation either to Congress or to the Member Banks of the Federal Reserve.

Economists point out that money loaned into existence can *never* be totally repaid, because only the *principal* was loaned into circulation but the *principal and interest* has to be payed back.

THE REAL STORY OF MONETARY CONTROL FOR AMERICA: BILLONS FOR THE BANKERS AND DEBTS FOR THE PEOPLE

Americans living in the richest nation on earth seem always to be short of money. Wives are working in unprecedented numbers, husbands hope for overtime hours to earn more or take part-time jobs evenings and weekends, children look for odd jobs for spending money, the family debt climbs higher, and psychologists say one of the biggest causes of family quarrels and breakups is "arguments over money." Much of this trouble can be traced to our present "debt-money system."

Too few Americans realize why our Christian Founding Fathers were Statesmen who wrote into Article I of the U.S.

Constitution: *"Congress shall have the power to coin money and regulate the value thereof."* They did this in prayerful hope that it would prevent the "love of money" from destroying the Republic they had founded. Subversion of Article I of the Constitution has brought on us the "evil" against which God's Word had warned.

MONEY IS MAN'S ONLY "CREATION"

Economists use the term "create" when speaking of the process by which money comes into existence. Creation means making something that did not exist before. Lumbermen make boards from trees; workers build houses from lumber and factories manufacture automobiles from metal, glass and other material things. But in all these they did not "create," they only *exchanged* existing materials into a more usable, and therefore more valuable form. But this is *not* so with money. Here, and here alone, man actually "creates" something out of nothing. A piece of paper, of little value, is printed so that it becomes of equal worth as a piece of lumber. With different figures it can buy an automobile or even a house. Its value has been "created" in the true meaning of the word.

CREATING MONEY IS VERY PROFITABLE

As seen by the above, money is very cheap to make, and whoever does the "creating" of money in a nation can make a tremendous profit and wield tremendous control in this world. Builders work hard to make a profit of 5% above their cost to build a house. Auto makers sell their cars for 1% to 2% above the cost of manufacture and its considered good business. But money "manufacturers" have *no limit* on their profits, since but a few cents will print a $1 dollar bill, or a $10,000 dollar bill!

AN ADEQUATE MONEY SUPPLY

An adequate supply of money is indispensable to civilized society. We could forego many *other* things, but without money industry would grind to a halt, farms would become only self-sustaining units, surplus food would disappear, jobs requiring the work of more than one man or one family would remain undone, shipping, and large movements of goods would cease, hungry people would plunder and kill to remain alive, and all government — except family or tribe — would cease to function.

An overstatement? Not at all. Money is the "blood" of civilized society, the means of all commercial trade except simple barter. It is the measure and the instrument by which one product is sold and another purchased. Remove money, or even reduce the supply below that which is necessary to carry on current levels of trade, and the results are catastrophic. For an example, we need only look at America's Depression of the early 1930's.

THE BANKERS DEPRESSION OF THE 1930's

In 1930, America did not lack industrial capacity, fertile farm land, skilled and willing workers, nor industrious farm families. It had an extensive and highly efficient transportation system in railroads, road networks, and inland and ocean waterways. Communications between regions and localities were the best in the world, utilizing telephone, teletype, radio, and a well-operated government mail system. No war had ravaged the cities or the countryside, no pestilence weakened the population, nor had famine stalked the land. The United States of America, in 1930, lacked only one thing: an adequate supply of money to carry on trade and commerce. In the early 1930's, Bankers — *the only source of new money and credit* — DELIBERATELY refused loans to industries, stores and farms to intentionally manufacture a "recession".

Payments on existing loans were still demanded, causing money to rapidly disappear from circulation. Goods were readily *available* to be purchased and jobs waiting to be done, but the forced lack of money brought the nation to a halt. By this simple ploy, America was put into a "depression" and the Bankers

TOOK possession of hundreds of thousands of farms, homes, and business properties. The people were told that "times are hard and money is short." Not understanding the *"system"*, the people were heartlessly robbed of their earnings, their savings, their property, and of even their lives.

MONEY FOR PEACE? - NO! MONEY FOR WAR? - YES!
World War II ended the "depression." The same Bankers who in the early 1930's had no loans for peacetime farms, houses, food and clothes, suddenly had unlimited *Billions* to lend for army barracks, K-rations and military uniforms! A nation that in 1934 could not produce *food* for sale, suddenly could produce *bombs* to send — for free! — to Germany and Japan. (More on this paradox at another time).

With the sudden increase in money, people were hired, farms sold their produce, factories went to two shifts a day, mines reopened, and "The Great Depression" was over, just like that! Politicians were blamed for starting the depression, and *other* politicians took credit for ending it.

The truth of the matter was: *lack* of money, caused by the Bankers, brought on the depression, and *adequate* money ended it. The people were never told that simple truth, and in future reports we will show how these same Bankers — who control our money and credit — have used their power and control to **"pillage America**," and put us *further* under their tyrannical control.

TELL THE PEOPLE
The "hidden" conspirators in politics, religion, education, entertainment, and the news media are working for a Banker-owned United States in a Banker-owned world under a Banker-owned One World Government!

Love of Country, compassion for your race, and concern for your children should make you deeply interested in this — **America's greatest problem** — because *our* generation has never suffered under the "yoke," as the coming generations will. Usury and taxes will continue to take a larger and larger part of the annual earnings of the people and put them into the pockets of the Bankers and their political Agents. Increasing "government" regulations will prevent citizens' protest and opposition to their control. Its possible that your grandchildren will own *neither* home *nor* automobile, but will live in "government-owned" apartments and ride to work in "government-owned" vehicles, both paying usury to the Bankers, BEING ALLOWED TO KEEP JUST ENOUGH OF THEIR EARNINGS TO BUY A MINIMUM OF FOOD AND OF CLOTHING, while their Rulers wallow in luxury! In Asia and eastern Europe it is called "Communism" — in America it is called "Capitalism and Democracy." America is not a Democracy, —**America is a Republic!**

"When God bids one uncover iniquity, in order to exterminate it, one should lay it bare; and divine Love will bless this endeavor and those whom it reaches. 'Nothing is hid that shall not be revealed'. It requires courage to utter truth; for the higher Truth lifts her voice, the louder will error scream, until its inarticulate sound is forever silenced in oblivion " — Mary Baker Eddy

Chapter 2
The Power To Coin Money

When we can see the disastrous results of an artificially created shortage of money, we can better understand why our Founding Fathers, who understood both money and God's Laws, insisted on placing the power to "create" money and the power to control it *only* in the hands of the Federal Congress.

They believed that *all* citizens should share in the profits of its "creation," and therefore the national government must be the *only* "creator" of money. They *further* believed that *all* citizens, of whatever State or Territory or station in life would benefit by an adequate and *stable* currency, and therefore the national government must be, by law, the *only* controller of the value of money.

Since the Federal Congress was the only legislative body subject to all the citizens at the ballot box, it was, to their minds, the only safe depository of so much profit and so much power. They wrote it out in the simple, but all-inclusive, statement: ***"Congress shall have the Power to Coin Money and Regulate the Value Thereof."***

HOW THE PEOPLE LOST MONETARY CONTROL TO THE FEDERAL RESERVE

Instead of the Constitutional method of creating our money and putting it into circulation, we *now* have an entirely *un*constitutional system. This has resulted in almost disastrous conditions, as we shall see.

Since our money was handled both legally *and* illegally before 1913, we shall consider only the years following 1913, since from that year on, *all* of our money has been created and issued by an *illegal method* that will eventually destroy the United States, if it is not changed!

Prior to 1913, America was a prosperous, powerful, and growing nation, at peace with its neighbors and the envy of the world. But in December of 1913, Congress, with many members away for the Christmas holidays, passed what has since been known as **The Federal Reserve Act**. (For the full story of how this infamous legislation was forced through our Congress, read *Conquest or Consent,* by W. B. Vennard). Omitting the burdensome details, without realizing the eventual consequences of its actions, it simply authorized the establishment of a Federal Reserve Corporation (the *non-federal* Federal Reserve Banks) with a Board of Directors (The Federal Reserve Board) to run it, — and the United States was divided into twelve Federal Reserve "Districts."

This simple but terrible law completely removed from Congress the right to "create" money or to have any control over its "creation," and gave that function to the *private* Federal Reserve Corporation. This was done with the appropriate fanfare and propaganda that this would *"remove money from politics"* — (they failed to add, *"and therefore from the people's control"*) — and prevent "booms and busts" from hurting the citizens of the United States. The people were not told then, and most still do not know today, that the Federal Reserve Corporation is a private for-profit corporation controlled by bankers, and is therefore operated for the financial gain of the bankers *over* the people rather than for the *good* of the people. The word "Federal" was used only to deceive the people.

MORE DISASTROUS THAN PEARL HARBOR

Since that "day of infamy" — more disastrous than Pearl Harbor — the small group of "privileged" people who loan us "our" so-called money have accrued to themselves all of the profits of printing our money, and more! Since 1913 they have "created" tens of billions of dollars in money and credit for themselves, which, as their own personal property, they then loan to our government and our people at interest. "The rich get richer and the poor get poorer" has become the *secret policy* of our Government. An example of the process of money-creation and its conversion into debt will aid our understanding.

THEY PRINT IT, WE BORROW IT, AND PAY INTEREST TO THEM!

Let's say, for instance, the Federal Government, having spent more than it has taken from its citizens in taxes, needs $1,000,000,000 to cover what it spent. Since it doesn't have the money, and Congress has given away their authority to "create" it, the Government must go to those whom it authorized to "create" it, for the $1 Billion. But the Federal Reserve, a private corporation, doesn't just *give* its money away! The Bankers are willing to *deliver* $1,000,000,000 in money or credit to the United States Federal Government in exchange for the Government's agreement (U.S. Bonds) to pay it back, with interest! So Congress authorizes our Treasury Department to print $1,000,000,000 in U.S. Bonds, which they then deliver to the Federal Reserve Bankers.

The Federal Reserve then pays the cost of printing the $1,000,000,000 (about $1,000) and makes the exchange.

The Government then *borrows* the money to pay its bills.

What are the results of this fantastic transaction? Well, $1 Billion in Government bills are paid, all right, but the Government has now *indebted* the people to the Bankers for $1 Billion on which we the people must then pay interest! Tens of thousands of such transactions have taken place since 1913, so that by the 1980's, the U.S. Government is indebted to the Bankers for over $1,000,000,000,000 (Trillion; 12 zeros!) on which the people pay over $100 Billion over that amount per year in interest alone, with no hope of ever paying off the principal! Supposedly, our children and the following generations will pay on it forever.

AND THERE'S MORE

You say, "This is terrible!" Yes, it is, but we have shown only *part* of the sordid story. Under this *unholy system,* those United States Bonds have now become *"assets"* of the Banks in the Reserve System which they *then* use as "reserves" to "create" *more* "credit" to lend. Current "reserve" requirements allow them to use that $1 Billion in bonds to *"create"* as much as $15 Billion in *new* "credit" to lend to States, Municipalities, to individuals, and businesses. Added to the original $1 Billion, they can have $16 Billion of "created credit" out in loans *also* paying them interest, with their only cost being $1,000 for printing the original $1 Billion! Since the U.S. Congress has not issued Constitutional money (money created according to the laws of the Constitution) since 1863 [for well over 100 years], in order for the people to have money to carry on trade and commerce, they are forced to *borrow* the "credit" created by the Monopoly Bankers, and pay them usury-interest!

AND THERE'S STILL MORE

In addition to the vast wealth drawn to them through this almost *unlimited usury,* the Bankers who control the money at the top are able to approve or disapprove large loans to large and successful corporations to the extent that a refusal of a loan will bring about a reduction in the price that the Corporation's stock sells for on the market. After depressing the price, the Bankers' agents *then* buy up large blocks of the stock, after which purchase the sometimes multi-million dollar loan is approved, the stock rises, and is then *sold for a profit.* In this manner billions of dollars are made with which to buy *more* stock. This practice is *so refined* today that the Federal Reserve Board need only announce to the newspapers an *increase* or *decrease* in their "rediscount rate," to send stocks *up* and *down* as they wish. Using this method, since 1913, the Bankers and their agents have purchased secret or open control of almost every large corporation in America. Using that control, they *then* force the corporations to borrow *huge sums* from their banks so that corporate earnings are *siphoned off* in the form of interest to the bank. This leaves little as actual *"profits"* which can be paid as *dividends,* and explains why stock prices are so depressed, while the *banks* reap billions in interest from corporate loans. In effect, the bankers get almost *all* of the profits, while individual stockholders are left holding the *bag* [not the *purse*].

The millions of working families of America are now indebted to the few thousand Banking Families for *three times* the assessed value of the *entire United States!* And these Banking Families *obtained* that debt against us for the cost of bookkeeping, paper, and ink!

THE INTEREST AMOUNT IS NEVER CREATED

The only way *new* money — which is not *true* money, but is *"credit"* representing a *debt* — goes into circulation in America is when it is *borrowed* from Bankers. When the State and people borrow large sums, we seem to prosper. However, the Bankers "create" only the amount of the *principal* of each loan, *never* the extra amount needed to pay the *interest.* Therefore, the *new* money never equals the newly *added debt.* The amounts needed to pay the interest on loans is not "created" and therefore does not exist! It has to come later from the productive labors of the people.

Under *this* kind of a system, where new debt always exceeds the new money no matter how much or how little is borrowed, the total debt increasingly outstrips the amount of money available to *repay* the debt. The people can *never ever* get out of debt! The people are enslaved!

An example will show you the viciousness of this usury-debt system with its "built-in" shortage of money.

If $60,000 of money is *borrowed,* $255,931.20 must be paid back! When a citizen goes to a Banker to borrow $60,000 to purchase a home or a farm, the Bank clerk has the borrower agree to pay back the loan *plus interest.* At 14% interest for 30 years, the Borrower must agree to pay $710.92 per month for a total of $255,931.20 for a $60,000 house. The clerk *then* requires the citizen to assign to the Banker the interim *ownership* of the property in case the Borrower does not make the necessary payments to pay the borrowed money back. The Bank clerk *then* gives the Borrower a $60,000 check, or a $60,000 deposit slip, crediting the Borrower's checking account with $60,000.

The Borrower *then* writes checks to the builder, subcontractors, etc., who in turn write checks. $60,000 of *new "checkbook" money* is thereby added to "money in circulation." However (and this is the fatal flaw of a usury system), the only *new* money created and put into circulation is the amount of the loan, $60,000. The money to pay the interest is *not* created, and therefore was *not* added to "money in circulation." So this *Borrower* (and all those who follow him in ownership of the property) must *earn* (take *out* of circulation) $255,931 — almost $200,000 *more* than he put *into circulation* when he borrowed the original $60,000! (By the way, it is this *interest* which cheats all families out of nicer homes. It's not that they can't *afford* nicer homes; it's because the Banker's *usury* forces them to pay for *four* homes in order to get one!).

Every new loan puts the same process in operation. Each borrower adds a small sum to the total money supply when he *borrows,* but the *payments* on the loan (because of interest) then deduct a much *larger* sum from the total money supply. There is therefore *no way* all debtors can *pay off* the money-lenders. As they pay the principal and interest, the money in circulation disappears. All they can do is struggle against each other, borrowing more and more from the money-lenders each generation. The money-lenders (Bankers), who produce nothing of value, slowly, then, but surely and more rapidly, gain a death grip on the land, buildings, and present and future earnings of the whole working population. Proverbs 22:7 has come to pass in America: ***"The rich ruleth over the poor, and the borrower is servant to the lender."*** No wonder God forbids interest on loans!

SMALL LOANS DO THE SAME THING

If you haven't quite grasped the impact of the above, let's consider a small auto loan for 3 years at 18% interest. Step 1: Citizen borrows $5,000 and pays it into circulation (it goes to the dealer, factory, miner, etc.) and signs a note agreeing to pay the Banker $6,500. Step 2: Citizen pays $180 per month of his labor earnings to the Banker. In 3 years he will take *out* of circulation $1,500 more than he put *into* circulation.

Every loan of Banker-created money [credit] causes the same thing to happen. Since this has happened millions of times since 1913, and continues today, you can see why America has gone from a prosperous, debt-free nation to a debt-ridden nation where practically *every* home, farm and business is paying *usury-tribute* to some Banker. The usury-tribute to the Bankers on personal, local, State and Federal debt totals more than the combined earnings of 50% (half) of the working people! Soon it will be 60% and continue upward!

THIS IS WHY BANKERS PROSPER IN GOOD TIMES OR BAD

In the millions of transactions made each year like those above, little actual currency ever changes hands, nor is it necessary that it do so; 95% of all "cash" transactions in the U.S. are by written check, so the Banker is perfectly safe in "creating" that so-called "loan" by writing his check or deposit slip, not against *actual* money, but *against your promise to pay* it back! The cost to him is paper, ink, and a few dollars in salaries and office costs for each transaction. It is "check-kiting" on an enormous scale! And the Banker's profits increase rapidly — year after year!

Chapter 3
The Costs Of The National Debt

THE COST TO YOU OF THE NATIONAL DEBT? — EVENTUALLY, EVERYTHING!

In 1910 the United States Federal debt was only $1 Billion, or $12.40 per citizen. State and local debts were practically non-existent. By 1920 — after only 6 years of Federal Reserve fantasy — the Federal debt had jumped to $24 Billion, or $226 per person. In 1960 the Federal debt reached $284 Billion, or $1,575 per citizen and State and local debts were mushrooming. By 1981 the Federal debt passed $1 Trillion and was growing exponentially as the Banker's *tripled* the interest rates. State and local debts are now MORE than the Federal debt, and with business and personal debts totaled over $6 Trillion, 3 times or more of the value of all land and buildings in the United States of America!

If we signed over to the money-lenders *all* the wealth of America, we would still owe them *more than 2 more Americas* (plus their usury, of course!).

However, they are too cunning to take title to everything. They will instead leave you with some "illusion of ownership" so you and your children will continue to work and pay the Bankers more of your earnings on ever-increasing debts. The "establishment" has captured our people with their ungodly system of usury and debt as certainly as if they had marched in with a uniformed army. Truly a Trojan Horse Takeover.

FOR THE GAMBLERS AMONG MY READERS

To grasp the truth that periodic withdrawal of money through interest payments will inexorably transfer *all wealth in the nation* to the receiver of interest, imagine yourself in a poker or dice game where everyone must buy the chips (the medium of exchange) from a "banker," who does not risk *his* chips in the game, but watches the table, and every hour reaches in and takes 10% to 15% of all the chips on the table. As the game goes on, the amount of chips in the possession of each player will go up and down with his so-called "luck", but the *total* number of chips available to play the game (carry on trade and business) decreases rapidly as time goes on. The game will eventually get low on chips, and some will run out. If they want to continue to play, they must buy or borrow more of them from the "banker."

The "banker" will sell (loan) them *only* if the player signs a "mortgage" agreeing to give the "banker" some real property (a car, a home, a farm, a business, etc.), in case he is unable to make periodic payments to pay back *all* of the chips plus some *extra* ones as "interest," The payments *must* be made *on time* whether he wins and makes a profit, or not.

It is easy to see that no matter how skillfully the players play, eventually the "banker" will end up with *all* of his *original* chips back, and — except for the very *best* players — the rest of the players, if they stay in the game long enough, will lose to the "banker" their homes, their farms, their businesses, perhaps even their cars, watches, rings, and the shirts right off their backs!

Our *real-life* situation is *much worse* than any poker game. In a poker game no one is *forced* to go into debt, and *any*one can quit at any time and keep whatever he still has. But in *real* life, even if we borrow *little* ourselves from the Bankers, the local, State, and Federal governments borrow *billions* in our name, squander it, then confiscate our earnings from us and pay it back to the Bankers *plus interest.*

We are *forced* to play the game, and none can *leave* except by death. We pay as long as we live, and our children pay after we pass on. If we *cannot* pay, the same government that obligates us to the debt sends the police to take our property and give it to the Bankers. The Bankers risk *nothing* in the game;

they just collect their percentage and "win it all." In Las Vegas and at other gambling centers, *all* games are "rigged" to pay the owner a percentage and they rake in millions. The private Federal Reserve Bankers' "game" is *also* rigged, and it pays off for them in billions!

In recent years, Bankers added *real* cards to their 'game'; "credit" cards are promoted as a *convenience* and a *great boon* to trade. Actually, they are ingenious devices by which Bankers collect 2% to 5% of every retail sale from the *seller,* and 18% interest from the *buyer,* — a real "stacked" deck!

YES! — IT'S POLITICAL, TOO!

Democrat, Republican, and Independent voters who have wondered why politicians always spend *more* tax money than they take in, should now see the reason why. When they begin to study our "debt-money" system, they soon realize that extravagant politicians are *not* the agents of the *people* but are the agents of the *Bankers* for whom they plan ways to place the people further-in debt. It takes only a little imagination to see that if Congress had been "creating" and spending, or issuing into circulation the necessary increase in the money supply — THERE WOULD BE NO NATIONAL DEBT — and the over $4 Trillion of other debts would be practically non-existent. Since there would be no *original* cost of money except printing, and no *continuing* costs such as interest, federal taxes would be almost nil. Money once in circulation would *remain* in circulation and go on serving its purpose as a medium of exchange for generation after generation and century after century, just as coins do now, with *no* payments to the Bankers whatsoever!

MOUNTING DEBTS AND WARS

But instead of *peace* and *debt-free prosperity,* we have ever-mounting debt and periodic wars. We as a people are *now* ruled by a system of Banker-owned "Mammon" that has usurped the mantle of Constitutional government from Congress and "we the people," disguised itself as our legitimate government, and set about to pauperize, enslave, and control us. It is now a centralized, all-powerful political apparatus whose main purposes are promoting war, spending we the people's money, and propagandizing to perpetuate itself in power. Our two large political parties have become its servants, the various departments of government its spending agencies, and the Internal Revenue "Service" its collection arm.

Unknown to the people, it operates in close cooperation with similar apparatuses in other nations as well, which are *also* disguised as "governments." Some, we are told, are friends. Some, we are told, are enemies. "Enemies" are built up through international manipulations and used to *frighten* the American people into going billions of dollars *more* into debt to the Bankers for "security", "military preparedness", "foreign aid to stop Communism", "minority rights", etc., etc. Citizens, deliberately confused by brainwashing propaganda, watch helplessly while our politicians give our food, goods, and money to Banker-controlled alien governments under the guise of "better relations" and "easing tensions."

Our Banker-controlled government takes our finest and bravest sons and sends them into foreign wars with obsolete equipment and inadequate training, where tens of thousands have been murdered or abandoned, and hundreds of thousands crippled. Other thousands have been morally corrupted, addicted to drugs, and infected with venereal and other diseases, which they bring back to the United States. When the "war" is over, we have gained *nothing*, but we are then scores of billions of dollars more in debt to the Bankers, which was the reason for the "war" in the first place!

AND THERE'S MORE

The profits from these massive debts have been used to erect a complete and almost hidden economic and political colossus over our nation. They keep telling us they are trying to do us "good" when in truth they work to bring harm and injury to our people. These would-be despots know it is easier to control and rob an ill, poorly-educated and confused people than it is a healthy and intelligent population, so they deliberately prevent real cures for diseases, they degrade our educational systems, and they stir up social and racial unrest. For the same reason they favor drug and alcohol use, racial intermarriage, sexual promiscuity, abortion, pornography, and crime. Everything which debilitates the minds and bodies of the people is secretly encouraged, as it makes the people less able to oppose it or even to understand what is being done to them.

Family, morals, love of Country, the Christian religion, all that is honorable is being gradually swept away, while they try to build their subservient New World man. Our new "rulers" are trying to change our whole racial, social, religious, and political order, but they will not change the debt-money economic system by which they rob and rule. Our people have become tenants and "debt-slaves" to the Bankers and their agents in the land our fathers conquered. It is conquest through the most gigantic fraud and swindle in the history of mankind. And we remind you again: The key to their wealth and power over us is their ability to create "money" out of nothing and lend it to us at interest. If they had *not* been allowed to do that, they would never have gained secret control of our nation. How true are Solomon's words: ***"The rich ruleth over the poor, and the borrower is servant to the lender."*** *(Proverbs 22:7).*

Almighty God warned in the Bible that one of the curses which would come upon His People for disobeying His Laws was: ***"The stranger that is within thee shall get up above thee very high; and thou shalt come down very low. He shall lend to thee, and thou shalt not lend to him; he shall be the head, and thou shalt be the tail."*** *(Deut. 28: 44-45).*

Most of the owners of the largest banks in America are of Eastern European ancestry and connected with the Rothschild European banks. Has that warning come to fruition in America?

Let us *now* consider the *correct* method of providing the medium of exchange (money) needed by our people. "When all else fails, read the Instructions."

THE CONSTITUTIONAL WAY: EVERY CITIZEN A STOCKHOLDER!

If we would have used the *Constitutional* way of "creating" the money needed in the nation, the Federal Congress would spend most of its time and study on the issuance and control of an adequate supply of stable money for the people. If an increase of population and production required an increase in the medium of exchange, *Congress* would authorize the "coining," (i.e., printing) of a prayerfully determined amount.

Some could be used to pay the current legitimate expenses of the Federal Government, with the balance paid directly to the citizens. Records for payment would be similar to Social Security records, except a citizen would be recorded at birth, instead of when he first goes to work. Each person on the records as of the date of the Congressional authorization would receive an equal amount just as if he were a stockholder holding 'one' share. Just think — a grant payment of only $20 to each citizen would put more than $4 billion of debt-free and interest-free money into circulation.

Such a suggestion always *scares* the Bankers. Their propagandists will *immediately* cry, "printing press money" and warn that it would soon be "worthless" and would "cause inflation"; when what we have now is printing press money by the non-federal Reserve that will soon be "worthless" and now is the cause of inflation.

The usury on their "created credit" (our debt) is the sole cause of "inflation." All prices — on all industry, trade and labor — must be raised periodically to pay the ever increasing usury charges. That is the only cause of higher prices. And the money-changers spend millions in propaganda to keep you from realizing that fact. The money-creators (Bankers) know that if we ever tried a Constitutional issue of debt-free, interest-free currency, even a limited issue, the benefits would be apparent at once. That issue they must not allow. Abraham Lincoln was the last President to issue such debt-free and interest-free currency, in 1863, and he was assassinated shortly thereafter.

NO BANKER'S PLUNDER

Under a Constitutional system of money supply, no private banks would exist to rob the people. Government banks, under the control of the people's representatives, would issue and control all money and credit. They would issue not only *actual* currency, but could lend *unlimited credit at no interest* for the purchase of capital goods, such as cars and homes. A $60,000. loan would require only $60,000. repayment, not $255,931 as it is now. Everyone who supplied materials and labor for that home would get paid just as they do today, but the Bankers would **not** get $195,931 in usury. THAT'S WHY THEY RIDICULE AND DESTROY ANYONE SUGGESTING CITIZENS-MONEY WITHOUT INTEREST AND WITHOUT DEBT.

History tells us of debt-free and interest-free money issued by governments. The American colonies did it in the 1700's and their wealth soon rivaled that of England's(!) and brought restrictions and demands from Parliament that led to the Revolutionary War. Abraham Lincoln did it in 1863 to help finance the Civil War. He was later assassinated by an agent of the Rothschild Bank, and **no debt-free or interest-free money has been issued in America since that time.** What a shame, with the solution to our money problems right at hand! What a shame, what a shame.

"If my people, which are called by my name, shall humble themselves, and pray, and seek my face, and turn from their wicked ways; then will I hear from heaven, and will forgive their sin, and will heal their land." — *2 Chronicles 7:14*

Chapter 4
Sound And Stable Money

DEBT FREE AND INTEREST FREE MONEY
 In addition to the early American colonies in the 1700's — whose wealth soon grew to rival that of England's, — several Arab nations issue **interest-free loans** to their citizens today. The Saracen Empire forbade interest on money for 1,000 years, and its wealth outshined even Saxon Europe. Mandarin China issued its own money, interest-free and debt-free, and historians and collectors of art today consider those centuries to be China's time of greatest wealth, culture and peace.
 Germany issued debt-free and interest-free money from 1935 onward, accounting for its startling rise from the depression to a world power in just 5 years! Germany financed its entire government and war operation from 1935 to 1945 without gold and without debt, and it took the whole Capitalist and Communist world together to destroy the German power over Europe and bring Europe back under the heel of the Bankers. Such history of money does not even appear in the textbooks of public (government run) schools today.
 Issuing money which doesn't have to be paid back in interest leaves the money available to use in the exchange of goods and services, and its only continuing cost is replacement as the paper wears out. Money is the "paper ticket" by which such transfers are made, and should *always* be in sufficient quantity to transfer all possible production of the nation to ultimate consumers. It is as ridiculous for a nation to say to its citizens, "You must consume less because we are short of money," as it would be for an Airline to say "Our airplanes are flying, but we can't take you because we are short of tickets."

SOUND AND STABLE MONEY

Money, issued in such a way, would derive its value in exchange from the fact that it had come from the highest legal source in the nation, our Constitutional Republic, and would be declared to be legal to pay all public and private debts. Issued by a *sovereign nation, under God,* not in danger of collapse, it would need no gold or silver or other so-called "precious" metals to back it. As history shows, the stability and responsibility of the government issuing it is the deciding factor in the acceptance of that government's currency — *not* gold, silver, or iron buried in some hole in the ground. The proof of this is America's currency today. Our gold and silver are practically gone, but our *currency* is accepted everywhere. But if the government was about to collapse, our currency would be worthless. Also, money issued through the peoples' legitimate government would *not* be under the control of a privately owned corporation whose individual owners benefit by causing the money amount and value to fluctuate, and the people to go into debt.

Under the present *debt-usury system,* the extra burden of usury forces workers and businesses to demand more money for the work and goods to pay their *ever-increasing debts and taxes.* This increase in prices and wages is called "inflation." Bankers, politicians and "economists" blame it on *everything* but the *real* cause, which is the *usury* levied on money and debt by the Bankers. This "inflation" benefits the money-lenders, since it wipes out the savings of *one* generation so they cannot finance or help the *next* generation, who must then *borrow* from the money-lenders, and pay a large part of their *life's labor* to the usurer. With an adequate supply of interest-free money, little borrowing would be required and prices would be established by people and goods, not by debts and usury.

CITIZEN CONTROL

If the Federal Congress failed to act or acted wrongly in the supply of money, the citizens would use the ballot or recall petition to replace those who prevented correct action, with whom the people believe would pursue a better money. Since the creation of money and its issuance in sufficient quantity would be one of the few functions of Congress, the voter could decide on a candidate by his stand on money, instead of the hundreds of lesser, and deliberately confusing subjects which are presented to us today. And since money is and would remain a national function, local differences or local factions would not be able to sway the people from the nation's (citizens') best interest. All other problems except the nation's defense would be taken care of in the State, County, or City governments where they are best handled and most easily corrected.

An adequate national defense would be provided by the same citizen-controlled Congress, and there would be no Bankers behind the scenes, bribing politicians to give $200 billion of American military equipment to other nations, disarming us while alien nations prepare to attack and invade the United States of America.

A DEBT-FREE AMERICA

With debt-free and interest-free money, there would be no high and confiscatory taxation, our homes would be mortgage free with no $10,000-a-year payments to the Bankers, nor would they get $1,000 to $2,500 per year from every automobile on our roads. We would need no "easy payment" plans, "revolving" charge accounts, loans to pay medical or hospital bills, loans to pay taxes, loans to pay for burials, loans to pay loans, nor any of the thousand and one usury-bearing loans which now suck at the life-blood of American families. There would be no unemployment, divorces caused by debt, destitute old people, or mounting crime, and even the so-called "deprived" classes would be deprived of neither job nor money to buy the necessities of life.

Criminals could not become politicians, nor would politicians become criminals in the pay of the Money-lenders. Our officials, at all government levels, would be working for the people instead of devising means to spend more money to place us further in debt to the Bankers. We would get out of the entangling *foreign alliances* that have engulfed us in four major wars and scores of minor wars since the Federal Reserve Act was passed, alliances which are now used to prevent America from preparing her own defense in the face of mounting danger from alien powers.

A debt-free America would mean mothers would not have to work. With many mothers at home, juvenile delinquency would rapidly decrease. The elimination of the usury and debt would be the equivalent of more than a 50% raise in the purchasing power of every worker. With this cancellation of all debts, the return to the people of all the property and wealth the parasitic Bankers and their quasi-legal agents have stolen by usury and fraud, and the ending of their theft of $300 Billion (or more) every year from the people, America would be prosperous and powerful beyond the wildest dreams of its citizens today. And we would be at peace!

Here is a Bible example of cancellation of debts to the money lenders, and restoration of property and money to the people:

"There was a great cry of the people and of their wives against their brethren... For there were that said, We have mortgaged our lands, vineyards, and houses, that we might buy corn, because of the dearth. We have borrowed money for the king's tribute, and that upon our lands and vineyards: and, lo, we bring into bondage our sons and our daughters to be servants; for other men have our lands and vineyards.

And I [Nehemiah] was very angry when I heard their cry and these words. Then I rebuked the nobles, and the rulers, and said unto them, Ye exact <u>usury</u>, every one of his brother.

And I said unto them, It is no good that ye do: ought ye not to walk in the fear of our God because of the reproach of the heathen our enemies? Restore, I pray you, to them, even this day, their lands, their vineyards, their oliveyards, and their houses, also the hundredth part of the money, and of the corn, the wine, and the oil, that ye exact from them.

Then said they, We will restore them, and will require nothing of them; so will we do as thou sayest. And all the congregation said, Amen, and praised the Lord. And the people did according to this promise. (Nehemiah 5:1-13.)

WHY YOU HAVEN'T KNOWN

We realize this small and necessarily incomplete article on money may be charged with oversimplification. Some may say that if it is that simple the people would have known about it, and it could not have happened. But this **MONEY-LENDERS'** *cons***PIRACY** is as old as Babylon, and even in America it dates far back before the year 1913. Actually, 1913 may be considered the pivotal year in which their prior plans came to fruition and the way opened up for the complete economic conquest of our people. This *cons***PIRACY** is old enough in America, that its agents have been for *years* in key positions as newspaper publishers, editors, columnists, church ministers, university presidents, professors, textbook writers, labor union leaders, movie makers, radio and TV commentators, politicians — from school board members to U.S. Presidents — and many others.

CONTROLLED NEWS AND INFORMATION

These agents control the information available to our people. They manipulate public opinion, elect whom they will locally and nationally, and never expose the crooked money system. They promote school bonds, municipal bonds, expensive and detrimental farm programs, "urban renewal," foreign aid, and many other schemes which will put the people more into debt to the Bankers. Thoughtful citizens wonder why billions are spent on one program and billions on another which may duplicate it or even nullify it, such as paying some farmers *not* to raise crops, while at the same time building dams or canals to irrigate *more* farm land. Crazy or stupid? Neither. **The goal is more debt for the people.** Thousands of government-sponsored ways to waste money go on thoughtlessly and continually every day. Many make no sense, but they are never exposed for what they really are, builders of **"Billions for the bankers and Debts for the people."**

So-called "economic experts" write syndicated columns in hundreds of newspapers, craftily designed to prevent the people from learning the simple truth about **our debt money-system**. Commentators on radio and TV, preachers, educators, and politicians blame the people as wasteful, lazy, or spend-thrift, and blame the workers, and consumers for the increase in debts and the inflation of prices, when they *know* the cause is **our debt money-system** itself. Our people are literally *drowned* in charges and counter-charges designed to confuse them and keep them from understanding the unconstitutional and **evil money-system** that is so efficiently and silently robbing the farmers, the workers, and the businessmen of the fruits of their labors and of their freedoms.

When some few Patriotic people or organizations who know the truth begin to expose the Bankers or try to stop any of their mad schemes, those people are ridiculed and smeared as "right-wing extremists", "super-patriots", "ultra-rightists", "bigots", "racists", even "fascists" and "anti-Semites". Any name is used which will cause them to shut up or will at least stop other people from listening to the warning they are giving. Articles and books are kept out of schools, libraries, and book stores, in the land of supposedly "free speech".

Some, who are especially vocal in their exposure of this **treason** against our people, are harassed by government agencies such as the EPA, OSHA, the IRS, and others, causing them financial loss or bankruptcy. Using the above methods, they have been completely successful in preventing *most* Americans from learning the things you are reading here. However, in spite of their control of information, they realize many citizens are now learning the truth. Therefore, to prevent violence or armed resistance to their **pillage of America,** they plan to register all firearms and eventually to disarm all citizens. They have to eliminate almost all guns, except those in the hands of *their* government police and army.

WHY HAVEN'T WE BEEN TOLD ALL THIS?

Why hasn't somebody told us about this scandal — **one of the greatest frauds in history** — that has caused Americans and others to spill oceans of blood, pay trillions of dollars in interest on fraudulent loans, and burden themselves with unnecessary taxation?

"Now the children of Israel came into Egypt; every man and his household came... And the children of Israel were fruitful, and increased abundantly... "Now there arose up a new king over Egypt, which knew not Joseph. And he said unto his people, Behold, the people of the children of Israel are more and mightier than we: Come on, let us deal **shrewdly** *with them." "And they made the children of Israel to serve with rigor: And they made their lives bitter with hard bondage in all manner of service in the field: all their service, wherein they made them serve, was with rigor." (Exodus 1:1,7-10,13,14).*

Many Americans today struggle from week to week to pay their bills while **Billions** of their money pass into other hands. An "enemy" has captured and enslaved our Great Land: America!

Chapter 5
What Famous Men Have Said

WHAT FAMOUS MEN HAVE SAID ABOUT THIS MONEY QUESTION

PRESIDENT THOMAS JEFFERSON: *"The system of banking is a blot left in all our Constitutions, which, if not covered over, will end in their destruction. I sincerely believe that banking institutions are more dangerous than standing armies; and that the principle of spending money, to be paid by posterity... is but swindling futurity on a large scale."*

PRESIDENT JAMES A. GARFIELD: *"Whoever controls the volume of money in any country is absolute master of all industry and commerce".*

CONGRESSMAN LOUIS T. McFADDEN: *"The Federal Reserve Banks are one of the most corrupt institutions the world has ever seen. There is not a man within the sound of my voice who does not know that this Nation is run by the International Bankers".*

HORACE GREELEY: *"While boasting of our noble deeds we're careful to conceal the ugly fact that by an iniquitous money system we have nationalized a system of oppression which, though more refined, is not less cruel than the old system of chattel slavery.*

THOMAS A. EDISON: *"People who will not turn a shovel full of dirt on the project (Muscle Shoals Dam) nor contribute a pound of material, will collect more money from the United States than will the People who supply all the material and do all the work. This is the terrible thing about interest... But here is the point: If the Nation can issue a dollar bond, it can issue a dollar bill. The element that makes the bond good makes the bill good also. The difference between the bond and the bill is that the bond lets the money broker collect twice the* *amount of the bond plus an additional 20%. Whereas the currency, the honest sort provided by the Constitution of the United States, pays nobody but those who contribute in some useful way. It is absurd to say our Country can issue bonds and cannot issue currency. Both are promises to pay, but one fattens the usurer, while the other helps the People. If the currency issued by the People were no good, then the bonds would be no good, neither. It is a terrible situation when the Government, to insure the National Wealth, must go into debt and submit to ruinous interest charges at the hands of men who control the fictitious value of gold. Interest is the invention of Satan".*

PRESIDENT WOODROW WILSON: *"A great industrial Nation is controlled by its system of credit. Our system of credit is concentrated. The growth of the Nation and all our activities are in the hands of a few men. We have come to be one of the worst ruled, one of the most completely controlled and dominated Governments in the world — no longer a Government of free opinion, no longer a Government by conviction and vote of the majority, but a Government by the opinion and duress of small groups of dominant men."* (Just before he died, President Wilson is reported to have stated to friends that he had been "deceived" and that *"I have betrayed my Country."* Here he was referring to the Federal Reserve Act passed during his Presidency.)

SIR JOSIAH STAMP (President of the Bank of England in the 1920's — the second richest man in Britain): *"Banking was conceived in iniquity and was born in sin. The Bankers own the earth. Take it away from them, but leave them the power to create deposits, and with the flick of the pen they will create enough deposits to buy it back again. However, take it away from them, and all the great fortunes like mine will disappear, and they ought to disappear, for this would be a happier and better world to live in. But, if you wish to remain the slaves of Bankers and pay the cost of your own sla-*

very, let them continue to create deposits".

ROBERT HEMPHILL (Credit Manager of Federal Reserve Bank, Atlanta, GA.): *"This is a staggering thought. We are completely dependent on the commercial Banks. Someone has to borrow every dollar we have in circulation, cash or credit. If the Banks create ample synthetic money we are prosperous; if not, we starve. We are absolutely without a permanent money system. When one gets a complete grasp of the picture, the tragic absurdity of our hopeless position is almost incredible, but there it is. It is the most important subject intelligent persons can investigate and reflect upon. It is so important, that our present civilization may collapse unless it becomes widely understood and the defects remedied very soon."*

THE APOSTLE PAUL: *"Owe no man any thing, but to love one another: for he that loveth another hath fulfilled the law. (Romans 13:7)*

WHO HAS NOT TOLD US AND WHY?

The politicians of the two parties, and other elected officials. All labor leaders. All economics and history professors at all colleges and universities. All financial newsletter publishers. All televangelists, your local minister, priest or rabbi. All "educational" groups like the League of Women Voters, the Heritage Foundation and the American Civil Liberties Union (ACLU). All news services, such as the Associated Press and the United Press International. All weekly "news" magazines, such as "Newsweek", "Time", and U.S. News and World Report. All daily newspapers, including the New York "Times" and Los Angeles "Times."

All of the above, and more, have hidden and are now hiding this truth from us! And — we might add, — even THE CHRISTIAN SCIENCE MONITOR!

And Why? BECAUSE OF FEAR!

THE COST OF FREEDOM

The cost of freedom runs high. We must be willing to pay its price — not in money, but in the essentials of what makes men, women and children, "Children of God"!

On the fourth day of July, in 1776, a small group of men, representing 13 colonies in the far-off Americas, boldly declared to the most powerful nation on earth, that they were independent and free. They declared, in radical terms, that "all men are created equal", endowed with certain "inalienable rights"; rights that government cannot take away, for government does not grant them.

In the Declaration of Independence, the founding fathers sought to demonstrate to the world that "the history of the present King of Great Britain, is a history of repeated injuries and usurpations, all having as a direct object the establishment of an absolute tyranny over these states." In the list, we find the basic philosophy for our Constitution and Bill of Rights.

It is often easy to simply blame faceless bureaucrats and politicians for our current state of affairs, and they do bear much of the blame. But a decent share rests with those of us who expect Washington, DC, to solve every problem under the sun. If we demanded that Congress abide by the Constitution, pass only constitutional authorizations and spending, while opposing the rest, politicians would be more responsive to our legitimate demands.

We have lost sight of the simple premise that guided the actions of our founding fathers. That premise? **The government that governs best is the government that governs the least.**

When we reduce the power of the federal bureaucracy, the costs of government will plummet. And when we firmly fix our eyes, undistractedly, on the principles of liberty, Americans will truly be free.

Ours is the freest land on the earth, and we enjoy a higher level of liberty than people anywhere. But this should never distract us from demanding *more* freedom and liberty. Freedom and liberty should be our forever motivation.

Whatever happened to the 56 men who signed the Declaration of Independence?

Five signers were captured by the British as traitors and tortured before they died. Twelve had their homes ransacked and burned. Two lost their sons serving in the Revolutionary Army. And one had two sons captured. Nine of the 56 fought and died from wounds or the hardships of winning the War. That's 29 of the 56, more than half.

What kind of men were they?

Twenty-four were lawyers and jurists. Eleven were merchants, nine were farmers and large plantation owners; well educated men of means. But they signed the Declaration of Independence knowing full well that the penalty, if they were captured, would be death.

Carter Braxton of Virginia — a wealthy planter and trader — saw his ships swept from the seas by the British Navy. He sold his home and properties to pay his debts, and died in rags.

Thomas McKean was so hounded by the British that he was forced to move his family almost constantly. He served in the Congress, without pay, and his family was kept in hiding. His possessions were taken from him, and poverty was his reward.

Vandals or soldiers, looted the properties of Dillery, Clymer Gwinnett, Walton, Heyward, Middleton, Ruttledge, and Hall. At the battle of Yorktown, Thomas Nelson, Jr., noted that British General Cornwallis had taken over the Nelson family home for his headquarters. Nelson quietly urged General George Washington to open fire. Nelson's home was destroyed, and he died broke.

Francis Lewis, too, had his home and properties destroyed. The enemy jailed his wife, and she died within a few short months.

John Hart was driven from his wife's bedside as she was dying. Their 13 children fled for their lives. His fields and his gristmill were laid to waste. For more than a year he lived in forests and caves, returning home to find his wife dead and his children gone. A few weeks later he died from exhaustion and a broken heart.

Norris and Livingston suffered similar fates.

Such were the stories and sacrifices of the American Revolution. These were not wild eyed, rabble-rousing ruffians. They were soft-spoken men of education and means. They had had security but they valued liberty more. Standing tall, straight, and unwavering, they pledged: *"For the support of this Declaration, with firm reliance on the protection of the divine providence, we mutually pledge to each other, our lives, our fortunes, and our sacred honor."*

These men gave you and me a free and independent America. The history books never told you a lot of what happened in the Revolutionary War. We didn't just fight the British. We were British subjects too at that time. We fought our own government! It was merely *based* in England.

Some of us take these liberties too much for granted. And this we should not do.

So, take a couple of minutes and silently thank these patriots in prayer. It's not too much to ask for the price they paid! Let's all remember and give thanks.

FREEDOM IS NEVER FREE!

As the scenes of the conflict "error" with "truth" are presented in a clearer light, the secret wiles of "mortal mind" are becoming now exposed and thereby successfully overcome. *"Surely in vain the net is spread in the sight of any bird. For we wrestle not against flesh and blood, but against principalities and powers, against the rulers of wickedness in high places"* (Proverbs 1:17; Eph. 6:12). But victory is assured for the elect of God, *"For the weapons of our warfare are not carnal, but mighty through God to the pulling down of strong holds; casting down imaginations [such as fear], and every thought to the obedience of Christ." (2 Cor. 10;4,5).*

MARTIN LUTHER, in the face of the Inquisition refused to recant — refused to back down in the face of death declaring, *"Here I stand; I can do no otherwise... So help me God!"* And in the face of that declaration, God did come forth to help mankind and a much needed Reformation was begun.

In the face of a bully we cannot run and hide, or we will *never* be free.

MARY BAKER EDDY — the Discoverer and Founder of Christian Science — once said to her stalwart friends at her beloved home in the New Hampshire hills — *"Go to the window and face the oncoming storm... And face it down!* This, in obedience, they did! And the tornado clouds dissipated and were blown away! (Mark 4.39).

America will not shake off her Banker-Controlled dictatorship as long as the people are *ignorant* of the hidden controllers behind the scenes. International financiers — who control most of the governments of the world and most information sources as well — have us completely within their grasp. They are afraid of only one thing: — **an awakened Patriotic Citizenry armed with the truth and trust in an almighty God!**

Chapter 6
How Things Came To Be

Most Americans do not know that the United Nations is at the head of a Great Conspiracy to destroy the sovereignty of the United States; and to enslave the American people within a United Nations one world dictatorship. This lack of knowledge regarding the frightening danger to our country and to the entire free world is simple. The masterminds behind this Great Conspiracy have absolute control of our mass media — especially television, radio, the press, and Hollywood.

The State Department, the Pentagon and the White House brazenly declare that they have the right and the power to manage the news — to tell us *not* the truth, but what they want us to believe. They seized that power on orders from the masters of the Great Conspiracy; and their objective is to brainwash the people into accepting their phony "peace" bait in order to transform the United States into an enslaved enclave of the United Nations Government of the World.

Many of our so-called "leaders" in Washington whom we elected to safeguard our nation and our Constitution are our betrayers. And behind them is a small group of elite men whose sole objective is the enslavement of humanity in the satanic plot of a One World Government. In order to give you a clear picture of this satanic plot, we must go back in time — back to the Millennium before Christ — and then come forward to the present day status of that plot.

Centuries ago a small group of elitists within the tribe of Judah chose to separate themselves from mankind and actively pursue a single-minded goal of world conquest — *no matter how long it takes.*

To give a proper background, we draw extensively on Douglas Reed's book, *The Controversy of Zion*. At one time Reed was a correspondent in central Europe for *The London Times.* As an author, he won international acclaim with books like *Insanity Fair*, *Somewhere South of Suez*, and *Far and Wide*. With the publication of *Far and Wide,* in 1951, Mr. Reed suddenly found himself banished from bookstores and publishers. He started *The Controversy of Zion* in 1951 and finished it in 1956, but it was not published until 1978 after Mr. Reed's demise.

In the Preface, he writes: *"There will have to be some signs that mankind is beginning to fight back against falsehood and suppression, and that he is reaching out for that kind of truth which, as the Bible tells us, "sets man free."* Such signs as he mentions began to appear several years before his death in 1976. All over the world, and especially in the United States since 1958, there has come into existence — as if at the command of God — numberless groups of intrepid articulate men, all locked in a struggle with what they see and feel to be an all pervasive evil threat to Western Christian civilization.

GOING BACK IN TIME

To understand the ramifications of what this Christian Republic and Christianity in general is faced with, we must go back to 950, or so, B.C., to when Israel and Judah were two of the twelve tribes descended from Abraham. Around this time, Israel chose to seek and follow the universal, loving God of all men while many Judeans chose the destiny of a race apart from men and to follow a *tribal* God of destruction and war.

These contradictory doctrines kept the two tribes apart for the next 200, or so, years until Israel was attacked by Assyria and disbursed, in 740 B.C. By 457 B.C. Judah had come under the domination of Levite priests who expanded the doctrine of a *separate* race into a "chosen" race. They that if the Judeans were obedient to all of the laws and judgments of God, they would come to rule over all people and be established in a promised land. This doctrine was infused with the precepts of self-separation from mankind, racial hatred, murder in the name of religious belief, and revenge.

These Levites were succeeded by the Pharisees, then by the Talmudists of Spain, the Rabbis of Russia, and finally by the Illuminati of today — propagators of the ideal nation, or global nation envisaged by the One Worlders Today.

THE PHARISEES OF ANCIENT TIMES

It was the Pharisees who formed an elite brotherhood, admitting only those who pledged themselves to strict observances of Levitical law. They were the earliest propagators of a secret conspiracy as a political science. They originated a basic method of controlling man that based on mutual suspicion and fear, by which conspiring groups are held together and made strong.

The Pharasees looked for a Messiah who would slay all their enemies and establish a political kingdom over all the peoples of the earth. This idea was unknown to the earlier Israelites who refused to accept the idea of a Master Race that the Levites expounded. When Jesus appeared and taught, "Love your enemies", it was a direct threat to the teachings of the Pharisees, who taught "hate your enemies." And reaching out to the universal God, men looked to Jesus for more light.

Perhaps the Judaic impulse in men was the reason why Jesus appeared among the Judeans where and when he did. The Judaic creed was tribalism in its most fanatical form, even at that time. And since every action produces an equal and opposite reaction, the reactive idea was bound to appear where the pressure was most great. In but a few words Jesus swept aside the entire mass of racial politics that the ruling sect had heaped upon the earliest moral law, and, like an excavator, revealed again what had been buried in the past.

A MOST DANGEROUS PROPHET COMES

The Pharisees at once recognized a most dangerous prophet

in their midst. Jesus' teachings appealed to the innate spirit of all men — that there is a universal God who lovingly cares for His people. This teaching posed a severe threat to the Pharisaical laws of the land, and if it continued to spread it would break the hold that the Pharisees held over the Judean Nation. The Pharisees accused Jesus of being a false Messiah, because he preached "Love your enemies" and "The kingdom of heaven is within you" in contradistinction to the Pharisaical laws which taught a future Messiah who would slay their enemies and establish His kingdom on the earth.

In a few words, the *Sermon on the Mount* dismissed hundreds of laws that the Levites taught. Only one of these views could prevail — thus Jesus was crucified. After the fall of Jerusalem, in 70 A.D., two distinct schools of thought emerged out of the Middle East. Christianity: preaching a Messiah that had come to save mankind; and Judaism: preaching a Messiah not yet come that is a vengeful God, who cares only for His chosen ones.

The Jewish Ghetto was a result of this Talmudic teaching. The Ghetto enabled the sect to maintain its hold on the people through fear. It is this fear that runs throughout the book of Deuteronomy. Deuteronomy offers material blessings in the form of territory, loot, and slaughter, in return for strict performance of hundreds of statutes and judgments — some of them enjoining even murder. The *Sermon on the Mount,* on the other hand, offers few material rewards, but teaches that moral behavior, humility, the effort to do right, mercy, purity, peaceableness and fortitude, will be blessed for their own sake and receive spiritual reward.

ELITISM ENTERS EUROPE

Toward the end of the 1700's, the destructive precept of elitism entered Europe in a new and fatal form — the French Revolution being the prime example. The assault was on all legitimate government, nationhood, and Christianity.

At about this time the Bavarian Government discovered the secret papers of Adam Weishaupt — a former Catholic priest. When these papers of Weishaupt's secret Society — the Illuminati — were seized in 1786, and published in 1787, the Blue Print of World Revolution and the existence of this powerful organization with members in high places was revealed.

The idea of leaguing men together in secret conspiracy and using them to achieve an aim which they do not always comprehend, pervades the entire mass of letters and documents the Bavarian Government seized. The Bavarian Government declared that the Weishaupt Documents were incontestably authentic. The existence of this Conspiracy has been affirmed by a long chain of authorities — by Edmund Burk, George Washington, and Alexander Hamilton, to name a few. George Washington, in private correspondence, declared that "The doctrine of the Illuminati has spread into the Unites States".

THE NEW WORLD REPUBLIC
In the New World, our Forefathers were ratifying a Constitution which proclaims that power resides in "We the People" — of a Republic whose foundation is based on the God given rights of individuals to rule the State. In the Old World, governments rests on the man-made right of the State to rule individual men, instead. The Illuminati sought rule by fear, the modern version of the destruction espoused by the elitist priests of Judah, centuries before.

America, by contrast, was founded on Christian principles. "We the People" as a nation have never sought to rule the world. Our Christian heritage has made this nation a Beacon Light to the world as the land of the free. Our forefathers had strong beliefs in God. Just as ancient Israel found its destiny intertwined with mankind, so too America — the restored Israel — found its destiny, as the melting pot of the world.

THE ILLUMINATI IS LAUNCHED
The satanic conspiracy was launched in the 1760s under the name of the "Illuminati."

Adam Weishaupt was a Jew who converted to Catholicism and became a Catholic Priest. Then — at the behest of the newly organized House of Rothschild — he defected to organize the Illuminati.

The Rothschilds financed the organization, and every war since then, beginning with the French Revolution, has been promoted by the Illuminati operating under various names and guises. We say, "under various names and guises" because after the Illuminati was exposed and became known, Weishaupt and his co-conspirators then operated under the cover of other names.

In the United States, right after World War I, they founded the Council on Foreign Relations (CFR), and the master minds in control are largely the descendants of the original Illuminati conspirators. But to conceal that fact, most of them changed their family names to American-sounding names. The true name of the Dillons, Clarence and Douglas Dillon — one of whom was the Secretary of the U.S. Treasury — is Lipowski. We'll come back to this later.

There is a similar establishment of the Illuminati in England named the British Institute of International Affairs. There are similar secret Illuminati organizations in France, Germany, and other nations operating under different names, and all these organizations, including the CFR, establish subsidiary or front organizations that are infiltrated into every phase of their various nation's affairs. But at all times, the operations of these organizations are master minded and controlled by the internationalist bankers who are controlled by the Rothschild elite.

THE ORIGINAL ILLUMINATI CONSPIRATORS
One branch of the Rothschild family financed Napoleon. Another branch of the Rothchilds — both branches the real masterminds of the Illuminati — financed Britain, Germany, and the

other nations in the Napoleonic Wars, and after the Napoleonic Wars, the Illuminati saw that the nations were so destitute, and so weary of war that they would accept any solution, so the Rothschild stooges set up the Congress of Vienna, and at that meeting they tried to create the League of Nations — their first attempted One World Government — on the theory that all the crowned heads of Europe were so deeply in debt to them that they would willingly or unwillingly, serve as their stooges. But the Czar of Russia caught the stench of their plot and completely torpedoed it. The enraged Nathan Rothschild — then the head of that dynasty — vowed that some day he or his descendants would destroy the Czar and his entire family, and his descendants did just that in 1917.

Bear in mind that the Illuminati was not set up to operate on a short-range basis. Normally a conspirator enters into a conspiracy with the expectation of achieving his objective during his lifetime, but this is not the case with the Illuminati. True, they hoped to accomplish their objectives during their lifetime, but — paraphrasing: "the show must go on" — the Illuminati operates on a very long-range basis. Whether it takes scores of years or even centuries, they dedicate their descendants to keeping the plot boiling until the Conspiracy is finally achieved.

BACK TO THE BIRTH OF THE ILLUMINATI

Adam Weishaupt was a Jesuit-trained professor of canon law teaching in Ingolstadt University when he defected from Christianity to embrace the Luciferian Conspiracy. It was in 1770 that the professional money lenders — the recently organized House of Rothschild — retained him to revise and modernize the age-old *Protocols of the Learned Elders of Zionism* which from the outset were designed to give the Synagogue of Satan, so named by Jesus Christ, ultimate world domination, so they could impose the Luciferian ideology upon the human race after a final social cataclysm to be caused by these satanic despots.

Weishaupt completed his task on May 1, 1776. This is why "May Day" is the Great Day of all Communist Nations even today. "Mayday" 1776 was the day Adam Weishaupt gave birth to the Illuminati, to execute their plan to conquer the world. A plan that requires the destruction of all existing governments and religions in the world. His objective is to divide the masses of people he called "goyim" (or human cattle) into opposing camps of ever increasing political, social, economic, and other controversial issues — the very conditions we have in our nations today! The opposing sides were then to be armed, and incidents provided to cause them to fight within themselves and destroy their national governments and religious institutions. Again, the very conditions in the world today!

THE ILLUMINATI PLANS

At this point, let us stress a prime feature of the Illuminati plans. Their blueprint for world control is based on the *Protocols of the Learned Elders of Zion* — (these Protocols are documented in a companion CS Monitor Special Report) — and they would do anything to divert suspicion from themselves. If you think this is far fetched, remember, they permitted Hitler to incinerate 600,000 Jews during the Holocaust.

Now, why did the conspirators choose the word, "Illuminati" for their satanic organization? Weishaupt himself said that the word "illuminati" is derived from the word "Lucifer" meaning "holder of the light." And his objective was to bring about a One World Government that would enable men with exceptional mental abilities to govern the world and prevent all future wars. Using the word "Peace" as bait — exactly as it was used in 1945 by the conspirators to foist the United Nations on Americans — Weishaupt recruited some 2,000 hired hands, the most intelligent men in the fields of arts and letters, education, the sciences, finance, and industry. He then established lodges of the Grand Order of the Orient (Masonic Lodges) to house their secret organizations. And in all this, he was acting under orders of the House of Rothschild.

THEIR INTENTIONS TO CONTROL

The Weishaupt plan required the Illuminati to use money and sex bribery to obtain control of men already in high places in government and other fields of endeavor. Once these influential men had been hooked by the lies, deceits, and temptations of the Illuminati, they were to be held in bondage and controlled by political and other forms of blackmail — threats of financial ruin, public exposure, physical harm, even death to themselves and their families. Many present top officials in our government in Washington are controlled in just this way by the CFR. Many homosexuals in our State Department, the Pentagon, and other federal agencies — even in the White House — are controlled this way.

Illuminati faculty in colleges and universities were to cultivate exceptionally bright students with international leanings, and recommend them for special training in internationalism. Such training was to be provided by granting scholarships to those students selected by the Illuminists. This gives you an idea of what a Rhodes Scholarship means. It means indoctrination into the idea that only a One World Government can end recurring wars and strife. This is how the United Nations was sold to the American people. One of the most notorious Rhodes Scholars in our midst today is William Clinton. His entire public record spells "Illuminati".

All such scholars were to be persuaded and convinced that men of special talent and brains have the right to rule the less gifted on the grounds that the masses do not know what is best for them, physically, mentally, and spiritually. In addition to the Rhodes and similar scholarships, there are special Illuminati schools located in Gordonstown, Scotland, Salem, Germany, and Athans, Greece. These three are the known ones. There are others that are not known. Prince Philip, the husband of Britain's Queen Elizabeth, was educated at Gordonstown at the instigation of Lord Louis Mountbatten, his uncle, a Rothschild relative who became Britain's Admiral of the Fleet after the end of World War II.

All influential people trapped under the control of the Illuminati — plus students who had been specially educated and trained — were to be used as behind the scenes agents to advise top executives to adopt policies which would, in the long run, serve the secret plans of the Illuminati's One World Conspiracy, to bring about the destruction of the governments and religions they were elected or appointed to serve.

Perhaps the most vital directive in Weishaupt's plan was to obtain absolute control of the press — at that time the only mass communications media distributing information to the public — so that all news and information could be programmed to convince the masses that a One World Government is the only solution to our many and varied problems. And do you know who owns and controls our mass communications media today? Practically all the movie lots in Hollywood are owned by the Lehmans; Kohn, Loeb & Company; Goldman Sachs; and other internationalist bankers. All the national radio and TV channels in the nation are owned and controlled by those same internationalist bankers. The same is true of each metropolitan newspaper and magazine chain, also of the wire services of the press, such as Associated Press, United Press International, etc. The supposed heads of all these media are simply fronts for the internationalist bankers who, in turn, compose the hierarchy of the CFR — today's Illuminati in America. Now can you understand why the Pentagon's press agents brazenly proclaim that the government has the right to lie to the people? What is really meant is that our CFR controlled government has the power to lie to, and be believed by, the brainwashed people of America.

BACK TO THE ILLUMINATI'S FIRST DAYS

Since Britain and France were the two great world powers of the late 18th century, Weishaupt ordered the Illuminati to foment the colonial wars, including our own Revolutionary War, to weaken the British Empire; and the French Revolution to bring the French Empire to its knees.

But in 1784, an Act of God provided the Bavarian government with evidence that revealed and proved the existence of the Illuminati, and this would have saved France from the French Revolution if the French government had believed it. In 1874, Weishaupt issued his directives for the French Revolution, and these directives were put into book form by A German writer, named Zwack. This book contained the entire Illuminati story including Weishaupt's plans. A copy of this book was sent to the Illuminati in France who were headed by Robespierre, whom Weishaupt had delegated to foment the French Revolution. The courier was struck and killed by lightning as he rode through Rallestadt on his way from Frankfurt, Germany, to Paris, France — and the police found the subversive book on his body and turned it over to the authorities. After careful study of the plot, the Bavarian government ordered the police to raid Weishaupt's newly organized Lodges of the Grand Orient and the homes of his most influential associates. All the evidence thus discovered convinced the authorities that the documents were genuine copies of the Conspiracy by which the Illuminati planned to use wars and revolutions to bring about the establishment of a One World Government, the powers of which the Illuminati — headed by the Rothschilds — intend to usurp as soon as it is established; exactly in accord with the United Nations plot of today.

In 1785, the Bavarian government outlawed the Illuminati and closed the Lodges of the Grand Orient, and in 1786, they published the lurid details of the Conspiracy. The English title of that publication is, *The Original Writings of the Order and Sect of the Illuminati.* Copies of the entire Conspiracy were sent to all the heads of church and state in Europe. But, the power of the Illuminati, which was actually the power of the Rothschilds, was so great that this warning was scoffed at and ignored. Nevertheless, Illuminati became a dirty word so it went underground. At the same time, Weishaupt ordered Illuminists to infiltrate into the lodges of Blue Masonry and form their own secret societies in all secret societies.

Only Masons who proved themselves internationalists and whose conduct proved that they had defected from God, were initiated into the Illuminati. Thenceforth, the conspirators donned the cloak of philanthropy and humanitarianism to conceal their revolutionary and subversive activities. To infiltrate the Masonic lodges in Great Britain, Weishaupt invited John Robison over to Europe. Robison was a high degree Mason in the Scottish rite. He was a professor of natural philosophy at Wittenberg University and secretary of the Royal Society of Edinburgh. Robison did not fall for the lie that the objective of the Illuminati was to create a benevolent dictatorship, but he kept his reactions to himself so well that he was entrusted with a copy of Weishaupt's revised Conspiracy for study and safe keeping. But because the heads of state and of church in France ignored the warnings given them, the Revolution broke out in 1789, as scheduled by Weishaupt.

To alert other governments to the danger, Robison published a book in 1798 entitled, *Proof of a Conspiracy,* but still his warnings were ignored — just as our American people have been ignoring warnings about the UN and the CFR.

THINGS ARE NOT ALWAYS AS THEY SEEM

There is documentary proof that our own Alexander Hamilton and Thomas Jefferson had been students of Weishaupt. Jefferson was one of Weishaupt's strongest defenders when he was outlawed by his government, and Jefferson brought the Illuminati into the then newly organized lodges of the Scottish rite in New England. This is why he was so insistent on founding the protections of our later Constitution.

In 1789, John Robison warned all Masonic leaders in America that the Illuminati had infiltrated into their lodges, and on July 19, 1789, David Pappen, President of Harvard University, issued the same warning to that year's graduating class, and lectured them on the influence Illuminism was acquiring in

American religion and politics. And, to top it off, John Quincy Adams, who had organized the New England Masonic lodges, issued his warnings. He wrote three letters to Colonel William L. Stoll, a top Mason, in which he alleged that Jefferson was using Masonic lodges for subversive, Illuministic purposes. Those three letters are in Wittenberg Square Library in Philadelphia.

A NEW STRATEGY COMES FORTH

The waylaid results of the Congress of Vienna created by the Czar of Russia, did not by any means destroy the Illuminati Conspiracy. It just forced the Illuminati to adopt a new strategy. Realizing that the one-world idea was for the moment killed, the Rothschild decided that — to keep the plot alive — they would have to heightening their control of the money systems of the European nations.

Earlier by ruse, the outcome of the Battle of Waterloo had been falsified when Nathan Rothschild spread the story that Napoleon had won. That news precipitated a panic on the stock market in England. All stocks plummeted almost down to nothing, and Nathan Rothschild bought the stocks for virtually a penny on the dollar of value. That trick gave him complete control of the economy of Britain and virtually of all Europe. So, as soon as the Congress of Vienna boomeranged, he forced Britain to set up the Bank of England, which he absolutely controlled. Even as later (through Jacob Schiff) he engineered the United States' Federal Reserve Act which gave the House of Rothschild secret control of the economy in the United States.

THE ACTIVITIES OF THE ILLUMINATI IN THE UNITED STATES

In 1826, a Captain William Morgan decided that it was his duty to inform all Masons and the public regarding the Illuminati and their secret intentions and plans — and to reveal the identities of the masterminds of the conspiracy plot — whereupon, the Illuminati promptly tried Morgan in absentia and convicted him of treason. They ordered an English Illuminist, named Richard Howard, to carry out their sentence of execution, of the "traitor".

Morgan was warned and tried to escape to Canada, but Howard caught up with him near the Canadian border — near the Niagara Gorge to be exact — where he murdered him. This was verified in a sworn statement made in New York by one Avery Allen, to the effect that he heard Howard render his report of the execution at a meeting of Knights Templars in St. John's Hall in New York. He also told how arrangements had been made to ship Howard's body back to England.

That Allen affidavit is on record in the Archives of New York City, NY. Very few Masons and fewer of the general public realize that general disapproval of that murder caused about half of all the Masons in the northern jurisdiction of the United States to secede. Copies of the minutes of the meeting held to discuss that matter are still in existence in safe hands and that secrecy shows the power of the masterminds of the Illuminati to prevent such historic events from being taught in our public schools.

COMMUNISM WAS ORIGINATED IN AMERICA!

Early in the 1850s, the Illuminati held a secret meeting in New York, which was addressed by a British Illuminist, named Wright. Those in attendance were told that the Illuminati was organizing to unite the nihilist and atheist groups with all other subversive groups into an international group to be known as the "Communists". That was when the word, "communists", first came into being and it was intended to be the supreme weapon and scare word that would terrify the whole world, and drive the terrorized people into the Illuminati One World Scheme. This scheme, Communism, was to be used to enable the Illuminati to foment future wars and revolutions. Clinton Roosevelt: a direct ancestor of Franklin Roosevelt, Horace

Greeley, and Charles Dana: foremost newspaper publishers of that time, were appointed to head a committee to raise funds for the new venture. Of course, most of the funds were provided by the Rothschilds. And, this fund was used to finance Karl Marx and Engels when they wrote *Das Kapital* and *The Communist Manifesto* in Soho, England. This clearly revealed that Communism is not a so-called ideology, but a secret weapon, a bogeyman agency of the Illuminati.

Weishaupt died in 1830, but prior to his death, he prepared a revised version of the age-old Conspiracy, the Illuminati, which under the various aliases was to organize, finance, direct and control all international financial organizations and groups, by working their agents into executive positions at the top. In the United States, we had Woodrow Wilson, Franklin Roosevelt, Jack Kennedy, Lyndon Johnson, Rusk, McNamara, and Fullbright, as prime examples.

In addition, while Karl Marx was writing *The Communist Manifesto,* under the direction of one group of Illuminists, Professor Karl Ritter, of Frankfurt University, was writing *The Antithesis* under the direction of another group. The idea was that those who direct the overall Conspiracy could use the differences in those two so-called ideologies to enable them to divide larger and larger members of the human race into opposing camps, so that they could be armed and then brainwashed into fighting and destroying each other, and, particularly, to destroy all religious institutions. The work Ritter started was continued after his death and completed by the German so-called philosopher Friedrich Wilhelm Nietzsche, who founded Nietzsche-ism. This Nietzsche-ism was later developed into Fascism, and then into the Nazism that fomented World Wars I and II.

In 1834, the Italian revolutionary leader, Guiseppe Mezini, was selected by the Illuminati to direct their revolutionary program throughout the world. He served in that capacity until he died in 1872. But, some years before he died, Mezini enticed an American general, Albert Pike, into the Illuminati. Pike was fascinated by the idea of a One World Government and ultimately he became the head of this Luciferian Conspiracy.

ALBERT PIKES BLUEPRINT FOR WORLD CONTROL

Between 1859 and 1871, Pike worked out a military blueprint for three world wars and various revolutions throughout the world, which he considered would forward the Conspiracy to its final stage in the 20th Century. Again, I remind our readers that these conspirators were never concerned with immediate success. They always operated on a long-range view. Pike did most of his work at his home in Little Rock, Arkansas, but a few years later, when the Illuminati's lodges of the Grand Orient became suspect and repudiated because of Mezini's revolutionary activities in Europe, Pike organized what he called "The New and Reformed Palladian Rite". He set up three Supreme Councils: one in Charleston, South Carolina; one in Rome, Italy; and the third in Berlin, Germany. He had Mezini establish 23 subordinate councils in strategic locations throughout the world. These have been the secret headquarters of the world revolutionary movement ever since.

Long before Marconi invented radio, the scientists in the Illuminati had found a means for Pike and the heads of his councils to communicate secretly. The discovery of that secret that enabled intelligence officers to understand how apparently unrelated incidents, such as the assassination of an Austrian prince at Sarajevo, took place simultaneously throughout the world and developed into a war or a revolution.

Pike's plan was as simple as it was proved to be effective. It called for Communism, Nazism, political Zionism, and other international movements to be organized and used to foment three global world wars and at least two major revolutions. The First World War was to be fought to enable the Illuminati to destroy Czarism in Russia, as vowed by Rothschild after the Czar had torpedoed his scheme at the Congress in Vienna, and to transform Russia into a stronghold of atheistic Communism.

Differences stirred up by agents of the Illuminati between the British and German Empires were to be used to foment this war. After the war would be ended, Communism was to be built up and used to destroy other governments and weaken all religions.

MAKING PLANS FOR WORLD WAR II

World War II, when and if necessary, was to be fomented by using the controversies between Fascism and political Zionism. And, here, let it be noted, that Krupp, the Warbergs, the Rothschilds, and other internationalist bankers financed Hitler — and the slaughter of some 600,000 Jews by Hitler didn't bother the Jewish international bankers at all. That slaughter was deemed necessary in order to create a worldwide hatred of the German people, and thus bring about the war against them. In short, this Second World War was to be fought to destroy Nazism and to increase the power of political Zionism so that the State of Israel could be established in Palestine.

During this World War II, international Communism was to be built up until it equaled in strength that of United Christendom. When it reached that point, it was to be contained and kept in check until required for the final social cataclysm. As we know now, Roosevelt, Churchill, and Stalin put that exact policy into effect, and Truman, Eisenhower, Kennedy, and Johnson continued that same exact policy.

AND PLANS FOR WORLD WAR III

World War III is to be fomented by using the so-called Communist controversies. Agents of the Illuminati, under whatever new name, are now stirring up the political Zionists and the leaders of the Moslem world. That next war is to be directed in such a manner that all of Islam and political Zionism will destroy each other, while at the same time, the remaining nations — once more divided on this issue — will be forced to fight themselves into a state of complete exhaustion, physically, mentally, spiritually, and economically.

Pike, himself, foretold all this in a statement he made to Mezini on August 15, 1871. Pike said that after World War III is ended, those who will inspire to undisputed world domination, will provoke the greatest social cataclysm the world has ever known. Quoting his own words, taken from the letter he wrote to Mezini and which letter is now catalogued in the British Museum in London, England, he said, *"We shall unleash the nihilists and the atheists, and we shall provoke a great social cataclysm which in all its horror will show clearly to all nations the effect of absolute atheism, the origin of savagery, and a most bloody turmoil. Then everywhere, the people forced to defend themselves against the world minority of revolutionaries, will exterminate those destroyers of civilization, and the multitudes, disillusioned with Christianity, whose deistic spirits will be, from that moment on, without direction and leadership, and anxious for an ideal, but without knowing where to send its adoration, will receive the true light through the universal manifestation of the pure doctrine of Lucifer, brought finally out into public view — a manifestation that will result from a general reactionary movement which will follow the destruction of Christianity and atheism — with both conquered and exterminated at the same time."*

When Mezini died in 1872, Pike made another Italian revolutionary, named Adrian Lemmi, his successor. Lemmi, in turn, was succeeded by Lenin and Trotsky; then by Stalin. The revolutionary activities of all those men were financed by British, French, German, and American international bankers — all of them dominated by the House of Rothschild.

THE INTERNATIONAL BANKERS OF TODAY

We are supposed to believe that the international bankers of today, like the money changers of Christ's day, are only the tools or agents of the Great Conspiracy, but actually they are the masterminds behind it all.

While the general public has been brainwashed by the mass

communications media into believing that Communism is of the so-called workers, the actual fact is that both British and American intelligence officers have authentic documentary evidence that international liberals, operating through their international banking houses, particularly the House of Rothschild, have financed both sides in every war and revolution since 1776.

Those who today comprise the Conspiracy, the CFR in the United States, direct our governments whom they hold in usury through such methods as the Federal Reserve System in America, to fight wars such as the Korean and Viet Nam Wars, created by the United Nations to further Pike's Illuminati plans to bring the world to that stage of the Conspiracy when atheistic Communism and the whole of Christianity can be forced into an all out Third World War on an international scale.

The headquarters of the Great Conspiracy, in the late 1700s, was in Frankfurt, Germany, where Mayor Anshelm, who adopted the Rothschild name, had established the House of Rothschild and linked together other international financiers who had literally "sold their souls to the devil".

After the Bavarian government's exposure in 1786, the conspirators moved their headquarters to Switzerland, and then to London. Since World War II — after Jacob Schiff, the Rothschild's boy in America, died — the headquarters of the American branch as been in the Harold Pratt Building in New York, and the Rockefellers — originally protégées of Schiff — have taken over the manipulation of finances in America for the Illuminati.

In the final phases of the Conspiracy, the One World Government would consist of a King-dictator, the head of the United Nations, the CFR, and a few billionaires, economists, and scientists who have proved their devotion to the Great Conspiracy. All others are to be integrated into a vast conglomeration of mongrelized humanity — actually slaves.

THE ONE-WORLD TAKEOVER PLOT

Now, let's see how our federal government and the American people have been suckered into the one-world takeover plot of the Illuminati's Great Conspiracy. And, always bear in mind that the United Nations was created to become the housing for that one-world so-called liberal Conspiracy. The real foundations of the plot for the takeover of the United States were laid during the period of our Civil War, not that Weishaupt and the earlier masterminds had ever overlooked the New World. As we have previously seen, Weishaupt planted his agents over here as far back as the Revolutionary War, but George Washington was more than a match for them then.

During the Civil War the conspirators launched their first concrete efforts. We know that Judah Benjamin, chief advisor of Jefferson Davis, was a Rothschild agent. We also know that there were Rothschild agents planted in Abraham Lincoln's Cabinet, who tried to sell him into financially dealing with the House of Rothschild, but "Old Abe" saw through the scheme and bluntly rejected it, thereby incurring the undying enmity of the Rothschilds, exactly as the Russian Czar did when he torpedoed their first League of Nations at the Congress of Vienna. Investigation of the assassination of Lincoln revealed that the assassin, Booth, was a member of a secret conspiratorial group. Because there were a number of highly important government officials involved, the name of the group was never revealed and it became a mystery, exactly as the assassination of Jack Kennedy is still a mystery today, but it will not for ever remain a mystery.

Anyway, the ending of the Civil War destroyed temporarily all chances of the House of Rothschild to get a clutch on our money system, such as they had acquired in Britain and other nations in Europe. I say "temporarily" because the Rothschilds and the masterminds of the Conspiracy never quit. So, they have to start from scratch, but they lost no time in getting started.

JACOB SCHIFF COMES TO THE NEW WORLD

Shortly after the Civil War, a young immigrant named Jacob H. Schiff arrived in New York. Jacob was a young man with a mission for the House of Rothschild. Jacob was the son of a Rabbi, born in one of Rothschild's houses in Frankfurt, Germany. We won't go deeply into his background. The important point is that Rothschild recognized in him not only a potential money wizard, but more important, he also saw the latent Machiavellian qualities in Jacob that could, as it did, make him an invaluable functionary in the Great One World Conspiracy. After a comparatively brief training period in the Rothschild's London bank, Jacob left for America with instructions to buy into a banking house, which was to be the springboard to acquire control of the money system of the United States. Actually, Jacob came here to carry out four specific assignments:

(1) Seize control of America's money system.

(2) Recruit men who, for a price, would be willing to serve as stooges for the Great Conspiracy, and promote them into high places in our federal government, in our Congress, into the U.S. Supreme Court, and all other federal agencies.

(3) Create minority group strife throughout the nation — particularly between the whites and blacks.

(4) Create a movement to destroy religion in the United States — Christianity being its chief target.

In regard to the first directive given to Jacob Schiff, to seize control of the United States money system, let's trace Schiff's steps to accomplish that end. As a first step, he had to buy into a banking house. It had to be the kind of a house which he could absolutely control and mould for that primary objective of seizing control of our U.S. Money system. After carefully scouting around, Jacob bought a partnership in a firm called Kuhn and Loeb. Like Schiff, Kuhn and Loeb were immigrants from German Jewish ghettoes. They came to the United States in the mid-1840s. Both started their business careers as itinerant pack peddlers. In the early 1850s, they pooled their interests and set up a merchandising store in Lafayette, Indiana, under the name of Kuhn and Loeb, servicing covered wagon settlers on their way west. In the years that followed, they set up similar stores in Cincinnati and St. Louis. Then they added pawn brokering to their merchandising pursuits. From that to money lending was a short quick step. By the time Schiff arrived on the scene, Kuhn and Loeb was a well known private banking firm, and this is the firm Jacob bought into. Shortly after he became a partner in Kuhn and Loeb, Schiff married Loeb's daughter, Theresa. Then, he bought out Kuhn's interests and moved the firm to New York, and Kuhn and Loeb became Kuhn, Loeb & Company, international bankers, with Jacob Schiff, agent of the Rothschilds, ostensibly the sole owner. Throughout his career, this blend of Judas and Machiavelli — the first hierarch of the Illuminati's Great Conspiracy in America — posed as a generous philanthropist and a man of great holiness, the cover-up policy set forth by the Illuminati.

THE FIRST GREAT STEP TO GAIN CONTROL

As we have seen, the first great step of the Conspiracy was to be the entrapment of our money system. To achieve that objective, Schiff had to get full cooperation of the then big banker elements in America, and that was easier said than done. Even in those years, Wall Street was the heart of the American money market and J.P. Morgan was its dictator. Next in line were the Drexels and Biddles of Philadelphia. All the other financiers, big and little, danced to the music of those three houses, but particularly to that of Morgan. All of those three were proud, haughty, arrogant potentates. For the first few years, they viewed the little bewhiskered man from the German ghettoes with utter contempt. But, Jacob knew how to overcome that. He threw a few Rothschild bones to them — said bones being the distribution in America of desirable European issues of stocks and bonds. Then he discovered he had a still more potent weapon in his hands, as the following shows.

In the decades following our Civil War our industries began to burgeon. We had great railroads to build. The oil, mining, textile and steel industries were outgrowing their swaddling clothes. All this called for vast sums of money, and much of that financing had to come from abroad. That meant from the House of Rothschild, and that was when Schiff came into his own. He played a very crafty game. He became the patron saint of John D. Rockefeller, Edward R. Harriman, and Andrew Carnegie. He financed the Standard Oil Company for "Rocky", the railroad empire for Harriman, and the steel empire for Carnegie, but instead of hogging all the other industries for Kuhn, Loeb and Company, he opened the doors of the House of Rothschild to Morgan, Biddle and Drexel. In turn, Rothschild arranged the setting up of London, Paris, European, and other branches for those three houses — but always in partnerships with Rothschild subordinates; and Rothschild made it very clear to all those men that Schiff was to be his agent-boss in New York.

Thus, at the turn of the century, Schiff held a tight control on the entire banking fraternity on Wall Street, which by then, with Schiff's help, included Lehman Brothers, Goldman Sachs, and other internationalist banks headed by men chosen by the Rothschilds. In short, that meant control of the nation's money powers, and he was then ready for the giant step — taking over and controlling our national money system.

THE NEXT GREAT STEP TO GAIN CONTROL

Now, under our Constitution all control of our money system is vested solely in our Congress. Schiff's next important step was to seduce our Congress to betray that Constitutional edict by surrendering that control to the hierarchy of the Illuminati's Great Conspiracy. In order to legalize that surrender, and thus make the people of America powerless to resist it, it would be necessary to have Congress enact special legislation. To accomplish that, Schiff would have to infiltrate stooges into both Houses of Congress — stooges powerful enough to railroad Congress into passing such legislation. Equally or even more important, he would have to plant a stooge in the White House — a president without integrity or scruples who would sign that legislation into law.

To accomplish that, he had to get control of either the Republican or Democratic Party. The Democratic Party was the more vulnerable. It was the hungrier of the two parties. Except for Grover Cleveland, the Democrats had been unable to land one of their men in the White House, since before the Civil War. There were two reasons for this: (1) the poverty of the Party, and (2) there were more Republican-minded voters than Democrats. The poverty matter was not a great problem, but the voter problem was a different story — but as we previously saw, Schiff was a "smart cookie".

THE VOTER PROBLEM SOLVED

This is the murderous method he employed to solve that voter problem. His solution emphasizes how very little the Jewish internationalist bankers care about their own racial brethren, as we shall see. Suddenly, around 1890, there broke out a nationwide series of pogroms in Russia. Many thousands of innocent Jews — men, women, and children — were slaughtered by the Cossacks and other peasants. Similar pogroms with similar slaughter of innocent Jews broke out in Poland, Romania, and Bulgaria. All those pogroms were implemented by Rothschild agents. As a result, terrified Jewish refugees from all those nations swarmed into the United States, and that continued throughout the next two or three decades, because the pogroms continued throughout all those years. All those refugees were aided by self-styled humanitarian committees set up by Schiff, the Rothschilds, and all the Rothschild affiliates. In the main, the refugees streamed into New York, but the Schiff/Rothschild humanitarian committees found ways to shuffle many of them into other large cities, such as Chicago, Boston, Philadelphia, Detroit, Los Angeles, etc. All of them were quickly transformed into naturalized citizens and programed to register as Democrats. Thus, all that so-called minority group became solid Democratic voter-blocks in their communities — all controlled by their so-called benefactors. Shortly after the turn of the century, they became vital factors in the political life of our nation. That was one of the methods Schiff employed to plant men like Nelson Aldrich in our Senate, and Woodrow Wilson in the White House.

MINORITY GROUP AND RACIAL STRIFE

At this point, let me remind you of another of the important jobs that was assigned to Schiff when he was dispatched to America. I refer to the job of destroying the unity of the American people by creating minority group and racial strife. By the pogrom-driven Jewish refugees into America, Schiff was creating one ready-made minority group for that purpose, but the Jewish people as a whole, made fearful by the pogroms, could not be depended upon to create the violence necessary to destroy the unity of the American people. But right within America there was a made-to-order, although yet sleepy minority group — the Negroes — who could be sparked into demonstrating, rioting, looting, murder, and other types of lawlessness. All that was required was to incite and arouse them. Together, those two minority groups, properly maneuvered, could be used to create exactly the kind of strife in America the Illuminati would need to accomplish their goals.

Thus, at the same time that Schiff and his co-conspirators were laying their plans for their takeover of our money system, they were also perfecting plans to hit the unsuspecting American people with an explosive and terrifying racial upheaval that would tear the people into hate factions and create chaos throughout the nation, especially on all college and university campuses, all protected by Earl Warren decisions, and our so-called "leaders" in Washington. Of course, perfecting those plans required time and infinitely patient organization.

DOCUMENTARY PROOF OF THE RACIAL STRIFE PLOT

Now to remove all doubts, let's take a few moments to look at documentary proof of this racial strife plot. First of all, they had to create leaderships and organizations to draw in millions of dupes, both Jewish and Negroes, who would do the demonstrating and commit the rioting, looting, and lawlessness. So in 1909, Schiff, Lehman and other conspirators organized and set up the National Association for the Advancement of Colored People, known as the NAACP. The president, directors, and legal counsel for the NAACP were white men — Jews appointed by Schiff — and this is the case to this very day.

Then, in 1913, the Schiff group organized the Anti-Defamation League of the B'nai Brith, commonly known as the ADL, to serve as the Gestapo and hatchet man outfit for the entire Great Conspiracy. Today, this sinister ADL maintains over 2,000 agencies in all parts of the country, and they advise and completely control every action of the NAACP or of the Urban League or all the other so-called Negro so-called civil rights organizations of the nation — including such leaders as Martin Luther King, Stokely Carmichael, Baird Ruston, and others of that ilk. In addition, the ADL acquired absolute control of the advertising budgets of many department stores, hotel chains, and TV and radio sponsors, also advertising agencies, in order to control practically all the mass communications media, and force every loyal newspaper to slant and falsify the news, to further incite and, at the same time, create sympathy for the lawlessness and violence of the Negro mobs.

THE TWENTIETH CENTURY AMERICAN MELTING PLOT

Here is documentary proof of the beginning of their deliberate plot to foment the Negroes into all their lawlessness. Around 1910, one Israel Zanquill, wrote a play entitled, *The Melting Pot.* It was sheer propaganda to incite the Negroes and Jews.

Because the play purportedly visualized how the American people were discriminating against and persecuting Jews and Negroes. At that time, nobody seemed to realize that it was a propaganda play; it was that cleverly written. The propaganda was well wrapped up in the truly great entertainment in the play, and it was a big Broadway hit. Now, in those years, the legendary Diamond Jim Brady used to throw a banquet at the famous Delmonico Restaurant in New York, after the opening performance of a popular play. He threw such a party for the cast of *The Melting Pot*, its author, producer and chosen Broadway celebrities. There fans met George Bernard Shaw and Jewish writer, Israel Cohen. Zanquill, Shaw, and Cohen created the Fabian Society in England, and had worked closely with a Frankfurt Jew named Mordecai, who had changed his name to Karl Marx. But, remember, at that time, both Marxism and Communism were just emerging, and nobody paid much attention to either, and nobody suspected the propaganda hidden in the writings of those three brilliant men.

At this banquet, Israel Cohen said he was then engaged in writing a book that was to be a follow-up on Zanquill's, *The Melting Pot*. The title of the book was to be: *A Racial Program For The Twentieth Century* At that time, everyone was absorbed in their own work, and, as significant as that title was, its real objective never dawned on anyone nor were they interested in reading his book.

DELIVERING AMERICA TO THEIR CAUSE

But, a newspaper clipping of an item published by the Washington, D.C. Evening Star in May 1957, was a verbatim reprint of the following excerpt from Israel Cohen's book, *"We must realize that our Party's most powerful weapon is racial tension. By propounding into the consciousness of the dark races, that they have for centuries been oppressed by the Whites, we can mold them to the program of the Communist Party. In America, we will aim for subtle victories. While inflaming the*

Negro minority against the whites, we will instill in the whites a guilt complex for their exploitation of the Negroes. We will help the Negroes rise to prominence in every walk of life, in the professions, and in the world of sports and entertainment. With this prestige, the Negro will be able to intermarry with the whites, and begin a process which will deliver America to our cause." This same excerpt was entered into the *Congressional Record* of June 7, 1957, by Representative Thomas G. Abernathy.

Thus, the authenticity of that passage in Cohen's book was fully established, but the one question which remained, was whether it represented the official policy or plot of the Communist Party, or was just a personal expression of Cohen himself. Hence, the need of more proof, and it was found in a pamphlet published in 1935 by the New York Communist Party's official Worker's Library Publishers. That pamphlet was entitled, *The Negroes in the Soviet America.* It urged the Negroes to rise up and form a Soviet state in the South, and apply for admission in the Soviet Union. It contained a firm pledge that the revolt would be supported by all American Reds, also called "liberals". On page 38, it promised that a Soviet government would confer greater benefits to Negroes than to Whites, and, again, this official Communist pamphlet pledged that *"any act of discrimination or prejudice against a Negro will become a crime under the revolutionary law."* That statement proved that the excerpt in Israel Cohen's book, published in 1913, was an official edict of the Communist Party and directly in line with the Illuminati blueprint for world revolution issued by Weishaupt and later by Albert Pike.

THE COMMUNIST REGIME IS CONTROLLED BY MASTERMINDS

Now, only one question remains, and that is to prove that the Communist regime is directly controlled by the American Jacob Schiff and London Rothschild masterminds of the Great Conspiracy. A little later we will see proof that will remove even the remotest doubt that the Communist Party, as we know it, was created by those masterminds, capitalists if you will. Note that Schiff, the Warburgs, and the Rothschilds planned and financed the entire Russian Revolution, also the murder of the Czar and his family, and that Lenin, Trotsky and Stalin took their orders directly from Schiff and the other capitalists whom they supposedly are fighting.

We can now see why Earl Warren and his co-Supreme Court Justices issued that infamous and treasonous desegregation decision in 1954. It was to aid and abet the plot of the Illuminati conspirators to create tension and strife between Negroes and Whites. We now see why the same Earl Warren issued his decision prohibiting Christian prayers and Christmas carols in our public schools. It was done to destroy Christianity.

We now see why Eisenhower, despite all the rigid Constitutional prohibitions against inferring in state law, sent federal troops into a Southern state to enforce the desegregation decision. Why Kennedy did likewise. And we now see why Johnson and 66 senators, despite the protests of 90% of the American people, voted for the Consular Treaty which opens our entire country up to Russian spies and saboteurs? All those 66 senators are 20th Century traitors.

IMPEACH AND THROW THE TRAITORS OUT

It is up to you and me — all American people — to force Congress, our elected servants, to impeach American traitors, and when proven guilty, they all should be punished as traitors who aid and abet our enemies; and that includes a rigid investigation of the CFR by Congress — and of all their fronts, such as the ADL, the NAACP, and SNIC. Such investigations will completely unmask the leaders in Washington and the Illuminati and all their affiliates as traitors carrying out the Illuminati plot. It will completely unmask the United Nations as the intended crux of the entire plot and force Congress to take the U.S. out of the

U.N., and throw the U.N. out of the U.S.A. In fact, it will destroy the U.N. and the entire plot.

Before we close this phase, we wish to reiterate and stress one vital point. Every unconstitutional and unlawful act committed by Woodrow Wilson, by Franklin Roosevelt, by Truman, Eisenhower, and Kennedy, et al, is now being committed by Clinton, directly in line with that same Illuminati blueprint for the takeover of the world. Also, the amazing treason by various members of our Congress has been committed on orders from the Illuminati CFR.

ENTRAPMENT AND TREASON, HAND IN HAND

Now, back to Jacob Schiff's entrapment of our money system and the treasonous actions that followed. This will also reveal the Schiff/Rothschild control of not only Karl Marx, but of Lenin, Trotsky and Stalin, who created the revolution in Russia and set up the Communist Party.

In 1908 Schiff decided that the time had come for his seizure of our money system. His chief lieutenant in that seizure was Colonel Edward Mandel House, whose entire career was that of chief executive and courier for Schiff, as we shall see. In the fall of that year, J. P. Morgan, John D. Rockefeller, Colonel House, Senator Nelson Aldrich, Jacob Schiff, Abraham P. Andrew, Henry Davison, Charles Norwood, Benjamin Strong, Frank Vanderlip, and Paul M. Warberg, and a few others, assembled in secret conclave at the Jekyll Island Hunt Club owned by J. P. Morgan at Jekyll Island, Georgia. In short, all of the international bankers in America — all of them members of the hierarchy of the Great Conspiracy.

A week later they emerged with what they later called the Federal Reserve System. Senator Aldrich was the stooge who was to railroad it through Congress, but they held that railroading in abeyance for one chief reason — they first had to plant their man, an obedient stooge, in the White House to sign the Federal Reserve Act into law. They knew that even if the Senate were to pass that Act unanimously, the newly elected President Taft would promptly veto it, so they had to wait.

In 1912, their man, Woodrow Wilson, was elected to the presidency. Immediately after Wilson was inaugurated, Senator Aldrich railroaded the Federal Reserve Act through both Houses of Congress and Wilson promptly signed it — and the Federal Reserve Act became law. That heinous act of treason was committed on December 23, 1913 — two days before Christmas when all the members of Congress — except for several carefully picked Representatives and three equally carefully picked Senators — were away from Washington for the holiday. How heinously treasonous was that act!

TO COIN AND REGULATE THE VALUE OF MONEY

Our Founding Fathers knew full well the power of money. They knew that whoever had that power held the destiny of our nation in his hands. Therefore, they carefully guarded this power when they set forth in the Constitution that Congress — the elected representatives of the people — would alone have that power. The Constitutional language on this point is brief, concise, and specific, and stated in Article I, §8, par. 5: — The Congress shall have the power *"To coin Money, regulate the Value thereof, and of foreign Coin, and fix the Standard of Weights and Measures"*. But on that tragic, unforgettable day of infamy, December 23, 1913, the men we sent to Washington to safeguard our interests — our Representatives and Senators and Woodrow Wilson — delivered the destiny of our nation into the hands of two aliens from Eastern Europe — Jacob Schiff and Paul Warberg. Warberg was a very recent immigrant who came here on orders from Rothschild for the express purpose of blueprinting that foul Federal Reserve Act.

THE NON-FEDERAL "FEDERAL" RESERVE

Now, the vast majority of the American people think that the Federal Reserve System is a United States government-owned agency. That is positively false. All of the stock of the Federal Reserve Bank is owned by the member banks, and the heads of the member banks are all members of the hierarchy of the Great Illuminati Conspiracy behind CFR. The details of that act of treason, which many traitorous so-called Americans participated in, are far too long for this thesis, but all of those details are available in a book, entitled *The Creature From Jekyll Island*, by G. Edward Griffin. In that book, Griffin tells the entire horrifying story, and backs it up with unquestionable documentation. Aside from it being a truly fascinating and shocking story of the great betrayal, every American should read it as a matter of vital intelligence for the time when the whole American people will finally become awake and smash the entire Conspiracy — and, with God's help, that awakening will surely come.

KARL MARX' PROGRESSIVE GRADUATED INCOME TAX

If you think that those aliens and their "by accident of birth" American co-conspirators would be content with just the control of our money system, you in for another very sad shock. The Federal Reserve System gave the conspirators complete control of our money system, but it in no way touched the earnings of the people because the Constitution positively forbids the withholding tax. But, the Illuminati blueprint for one-world enslavement called for the confiscation of all private property and control of individual earning powers. This — and Karl Marx stressed that feature in his blueprint — had to be accomplished by a progressive graduated income tax. As stated, such a tax could not lawfully be imposed upon the American people. It is succinctly and expressly forbidden by our Constitution. Thus, only an Amendment to the Constitution could give the federal government such confiscatory powers. Well, that too was not an insurmountable problem for the Machiavellian plotters. The same elected leaders in both Houses of Congress and the same Mr. Woodrow Wilson who signed the infamous Federal Reserve

Act into law amended the Constitution to make the federal income tax, known as the 16th Amendment, a law of the land. Both are illegal under Constitution. But the same traitors signed both betrayals — the Federal Reserve Act and the 16th Amendment — into law. And nobody ever realized that the 16th Amendment was set up to rob the people of their earnings, via inflation and the "Marxian" income tax.

Chapter 7
How Things Are Now

The Plotters didn't fully use the Federal Reserve Act until World War II when that great "humanitarian", Franklin D. Roosevelt, applied a 20% withholding tax on all small wage earners and up to 90% on higher incomes. Oh, of course, he faithfully promised that it would be only for the duration of the war, but what was a promise to such a charlatan who in 1940, when he was running for his third term, kept proclaiming, *"I'll say again and again and again — that I will never send American boys to fight on foreign soil."* Remember? He was proclaiming that, even as he was preparing to plunge us into World War II by enticing the Japanese into that sneak attack on Pearl Harbor to furnish him with his excuse.

And let us remind our readers that another charlatan named Woodrow Wilson had used exactly that same campaign slogan in 1916. His slogan was *"Re-elect the man who will keep your sons out of the war"* — exactly the same formula, exactly the same promise!

LICENSE TO STEAL

But wait — "You ain't heard nothin' yet!" That 16th Amendment income tax trap was intended to confiscate —*steal* — the earnings only of the common herd, you and me. It was not intended to even touch the huge incomes of the Illuminati gang — the Rockefellers, the Carnegies, the Lehmans, and all the other conspirators. So together with that 16th Amendment they created the tax-free foundation that would enable the conspirators to transform their huge wealth into such so-called "foundations" and avoid payment of virtually *all* income taxes.

The excuse for it was that the earnings of those tax-free foundations would be devoted to "humanitarian" philanthropy, so we now have the several Rockefeller foundations, the Carnegie Endowment Fund, the Ford Foundation, the Mellon Foundation and hundreds of similar tax-free foundations. And what kind of philanthropy do these foundations support? Well, they finance all the civil rights and protest groups that are creating all the chaos and rioting all over the country, like the Martin Luther Kings, etc.

The Ford Foundation finances organization like the Center for the Study of Democratic Institutions in Santa Barbara, commonly referred to as "Moscow West" and which was headed by "wonder boy" Hutchins, Walter Reuther, Erwin Canham, and others of that ilk. In short, the tax-free foundations finance those who are doing the job for the Illuminati's Great Conspiracy.

And what of the hundreds of billions of dollars they confiscate from the earnings of the common herd — you and me — used for? Well, for one thing, there's the foreign aid gimmick which gives billions to Communist nations, plus gifts of hundreds of jet planes, many of which were turned over to Castro, plus the training of Communist pilots so that they can better shoot down our planes; billions to "Red" Poland; billions to India; billions to Sukarno; billions to other enemies of the United States — that's what that the treasonously railroaded 16th Amendment has done to our nation, to the American people, to you and to me, to our children and their children to come.

Our CFR Illuminati controlled federal government can grant tax-free status to all foundations and pro-Red one-world outfits, such as the Fund for the Republic, but if you or a patriotic pro-organization are too outspoken or pro-American, they can terrify and intimidate you by finding a misplaced comma in your income tax report and by threatening you with penalties, fines, and even prison.

HOW NAIVE, HOW NAIVE!

Future historians will wonder how the American people could have been so naïve and stupid as to have permitted such audaciously brazen acts of treason as the Federal Reserve Act and the 16th Amendment. Well, we were not naïve and we were not stupid — we trusted the men we elected to safeguard our country and our people and we didn't have an inkling about either betrayal until after each one had been accomplished. It was the Illuminati controlled mass communications media that kept and is keeping our people naïve — even stupid — and unaware of the treason being committed against our country. Now, the big question is — when will we, the people wake up?

THE FINAL STEPS TO A ONE WORLD GOVERNMENT

Now, let's go back to the events that followed the rape of our Constitution by the passage of our Federal Reserve Act and the 16th Amendment in 1913. With Wilson completely under their control, the masterminds of the Great Conspiracy put into motion their next, and what they hoped would be their final steps to achieve their One World Government.

THE INTENTIONAL DEVISING OF WAR

The first of those steps was to be World War I. Why war? Simple — the only excuse for a One World Government is that it will supposedly ensure "peace". The only thing that can make people cry for that peace is war. War brings chaos, destruction, and exhaustion to winners as well as to losers. It brings economic ruin to both. Most importantly, it destroys the flower of the young manhood of both. To the saddened and heartbroken oldsters — the mothers and fathers who are left with nothing but memories of their beloved sons — peace becomes worth *any* price, and is the emotion upon which the conspirators depend for the success of their satanic plot.

Throughout the 19th century, from 1814 to 1914, the world as a whole was at peace. Such wars as the Franco-Prussian War, our own Civil War, the Russo-Japanese War, were what might be termed local disturbances that did not affect the rest of the world. All the great nations were prosperous. The people were staunchly nationalistic and fiercely proud of their sovereignties. It was utterly unthinkable that the French and the German peoples would be willing to live under a One World Government, or the Turks and the Russians, or the Chinese and the Japanese.

Even more unthinkable was that a Kaiser Wilhelm or a Franz Joseph, or a Czar Nicholas, or any monarch would willingly and meekly surrender his throne to a One World Government, but bear in mind that the peoples in all nations are the real power, and only one thing — war — could make the peoples of the nations yearn and clamor for a peace-ensuring One World Government.

But, it would have to be a frightful and horribly devastating war. It could not be just a local war between two nations. It would have to be a "world war". No major nation must be left untouched by the horrors and devastation of such a war. The cry for peace must be made universal. Actually, that was the format set by the Illuminati and Nathan Rothschild at the turn of the 19th century. They first maneuvered all of Europe into the Napoleonic wars — then, the Congress of Vienna, which they and the Rothschilds planned to transform into a League of Nations that would have been the housing for a One World Government — just as the present United Nations was set up to be the housing for the forthcoming, God forbid, One World Government.

Anyway, that was the format that the House of Rothschild and Jacob Schiff decided to employ to achieve their objective in 1914. Of course, they knew that that same format had failed in 1814, but they theorized that that was only because the Czar of Russia had torpedoed that scheme, while the present 1914 conspirators would eliminate that 1814 "fly in the ointment". They would make sure that after the new world war they were conspiring, there would be no Czar of Russia around to throw a monkey wrench in to destroy the machinery.

SMALL BEGINNINGS, GROSS ENDINGS

We won't go into how they accomplished this first step to launch a world war. History records that World War I was precipitated by a trivial incident, the kind of incident that both Weishaupt and Albert Pike had incorporated in their blueprints. That incident was the assassination of an Austrian, Archduke Ferdinand, arranged by the Illuminati masterminds. The war followed. It involved Germany, Austria, Hungary, and their allies (the so-called Axis powers) against France, Britain and Russia, called the Allies — only the United States was not involved during the first two years. By 1917, the conspirators had achieved their primary objective — all of Europe was in a state of destitution, all the peoples were war weary and crying for peace, and the outcome, too, was all set. It was to come as soon as the United States would be hurled in on the side of the Allies, and that was all arranged to happen immediately after Wilson's re-election. After that, there could only be one outcome — complete victory for the Allies.

THE BEST LAID PLANS OF MICE AND MEN

To fully confirm our statement that long before 1917 the Conspiracy headed in America by Jacob Schiff had it all set to hurl the United States in the war, we will cite the proof.

When Wilson was campaigning for re-election in 1916, his chief appeal was *"Re-elect the man who will keep your sons out of the war"*. But, during that same campaign, the Republican Party publicly charged that Wilson had long committed himself to throw us into war. They charged that if he would be defeated, he would accomplish that act during his two remaining months in office, but if re-elected, he would hold off until after re-election. But at that time, the American people looked upon Wilson as a "god-man". Well, Wilson was re-elected and as per the schedule of the conspirators, he hurled us into the war in 1917. He used the sinking of the Lusitania as an excuse — a tragedy that also was pre-arranged. Roosevelt, a "god-man" in the eyes of the American people, followed the same technique in 1941 when he used the pre-arranged Pearl Harbor attack as his excuse for hurling us into World War II.

Now, exactly as the conspirators planned, victory for the Allies would eliminate all the monarchs of the defeated nations and leave all their peoples leaderless, confused, bewildered and perfectly conditioned for the One World Government the Great Conspiracy intended would follow. But, there still would be an obstacle — the same obstacle that had balked the Illuminati and Rothschild at the Congress of Vienna peace gathering, after the Napoleonic Wars. Russia would be on the winning side this time as it was in 1814; therefore, the Czar would be securely on his throne. Here it is pertinent to note that Russia, under the Czarist regime, had been the *one* country in which the Illuminati had never made any headway, nor had the Rothschilds ever been able to infiltrate Russian banking interests. Thus, a winning Czar would be more difficult than ever to cope with, even if he could be enticed into a so-called League of Nations. It was a foregone conclusion that he would never go for a One World Government.

So, even before the outbreak of World War I, the conspirators had a plan in the making to carry out Nathan Rothschild's vow of 1814 to destroy the Czar and murder all possible royal heirs to the throne, and it would have to be done before the close of the war, and the Russian Bolsheviki were to be their instruments in this particular plot.

From the turn of the century, the chiefs of the Bolsheviki were Nicolai Lenin, Leon Trotsky, and later Joseph Stalin. Of course, those were not their true family names. Prior to the outbreak of the war, Lenin was headquartered in Paris. After the outbreak, Switzerland became his haven. Trotsky's headquarters was on the lower East Side in New York — largely the habitat of Russian Jewish refugees. Both Lenin and Trotsky were similarly bewhiskered and unkempt. In those days, that was the badge of Bolshevism. Both lived well yet neither had a regular occupation. Neither had any visible means of support yet both always had plenty of money.

All those mysteries were solved in 1917. Right from the outset of the war, strange and mysterious goings-on were taking place in New York. Night after night, Trotsky darted furtively in and out of Jacob Schiff's palatial mansion, and in the dim of those same nights, there were gatherings of hoodlums of New York's Lower East Side, all of them Russian refugees, at Trotsky's headquarters, all going through some sort of mysterious training process. But, it was all shrouded in mystery. Nobody talked, although it did leak out that Schiff was financing all of Trotsky's activities. Then, suddenly Trotsky vanished. So did approximately three hundred of his trained hoodlums. Actually they were on the high seas in a Schiff chartered ship bound for a rendezvous with Lenin and his gang in Switzerland, and on that ship was $20,000,000 in gold — the $20,000,000 Schiff provided to finance the Bolshevik takeover of Russia.

In anticipation of Trotsky's arrival, Lenin prepared to throw a party in his Switzerland hideaway. Men of the very highest places in the world were to be guests at that party. Among them was the mysterious Colonel Edward Mandel House, Woodrow Wilson's mentor and "palsy-walsy" — and more importantly, Schiff's special and confidential messenger. Another of the expectant guests was Paul Warberg of the Warberg banking clan in Germany who was financing the Kaiser and whom the Kaiser had rewarded by making him Chief of the Secret Police of Germany. In addition, there were the Rothschilds of London and Paris, also Lukinoff, Gaganovich, and Stalin, who was then head of a gang of train and bank-robbing bandits — he was known as the "Jesse James of the Urals". And, here we must point out that England and France were then long in war with Germany, and that on February 3, 1917, Wilson had broken off all diplomatic relations with Germany. Therefore, Warberg, Colonel House, the Rothschilds and all those others were supposed enemies, but of course Switzerland was neutral ground where enemies could meet and be friends, especially if they had some important scheme in common.

That Lenin party was very nearly ruined by an unforeseen incident. The Schiff chartered ship on its way to Switzerland was intercepted and taken into custody by a British warship, but Schiff quickly rushed orders to President Wilson to order the British to release the ship intact with the Trotsky hoodlums and the gold. Mission obeyed. He warned the British that if they refused to release the ship, the United States would not enter the war in April as he had faithfully promised a year earlier. The British heeded the warning, Trotsky arrived in Switzerland, and the Lenin party went off as scheduled.

But, they still faced what ordinarily would have been an insurmountable obstacle of getting the Lenin-Trotsky band of terrorists across the border into Russia. Well, that's where "brother" Warberg, Chief of the Germany Secret Police, came in. He loaded all those thugs into steel-plated cars and made all the necessary arrangements for their secret entry into Russia. The rest is history. The revolution in Russia took place and all members of the royal Romanoff family were murdered.

COMMUNISM IS A "VITAL" TOOL

Now, our chief objective is to establish beyond even the remotest doubt that Communism, so-called, is an integral part of the Illuminati's Great Conspiracy for the enslavement of the entire world — that Communism, so-called, is merely their weapon and bogeyman word to terrify the peoples of the whole world, and that the conquest of Russia and the creation of Communism was in great part organized by Schiff and the other international bankers right in our own back yard in the American City of New York.

A fantastic story? — Yes! Some might even refuse to believe it. Well, for the benefit of any doubting Thomas, we will point out that a number of years ago, Charlie Knickerbocker, a

Hearst newspaper columnist, published an interview with John Schiff, grandson of Jacob Schiff, in which young Schiff confirmed the entire story and named the figure "Old Jacob" contributed — $20 million dollars. If anybody still has a remote doubt that the entire menace of Communism was created by the masterminds of the Great Conspiracy, right in our own American City of New York, we will cite the following historical fact. All records show that when Lenin and Trotsky engineered the capture of Russia, they operated as heads of the Bolshevik Party. Now, Bolshevism is a purely Russian word. The masterminds realized that Bolshevism could never be sold as an ideology to any but the Russian people, so in April, 1918, Jacob Schiff dispatched Colonel House to Moscow with orders to Lenin, Trotsky, and Stalin to change the name of their regime to the Communist Party and to adopt the Karl Marx Manifesto as the Constitution of the Communist Party. Lenin, Trotsky and Stalin obeyed and that year of 1918 was when the Communist Party and the menace of Communism first came into being. All this is confirmed in Webster's Collegiate Dictionary, 5th Edition. In short, Communism was a tool created by the capitalists.

Thus, until November 11, 1918, the entire fiendish plan of the conspirators worked perfectly. All the great nations, including the United States, were war weary, devastated and mourning their dead. Peace was the great universal desire. Thus, when it was proposed by Wilson to set up a League of Nations to ensure peace, all the great nations, with no Russian Czar to stay in their way, jumped on that bandwagon without even stopping to read the fine print in that "insurance policy; that is, all but one — the United States — the very one that Schiff and his co-conspirators least expected would balk, and that was their one fatal mistake in that early plot. You see, when Schiff planted Woodrow Wilson in the White House, the conspirators assumed that they had the United States in the proverbial "bag". Wilson had been perfectly built up as a great humanitarian. He supposedly became established as a "god-man" with the American people. There was every reason for the conspirators to have believed that he would easily horn-swaggle Congress into buying the League of Nations sight unseen, exactly as the Congress of 1945 later bought the United Nations fiasco sight unseen. But there was one man in the Senate in 1918 who saw through that scheme just as the Russian Czar did in 1814. He was a man of great political stature, almost as great as that of Teddy Roosevelt and fully as astute. He was highly respected and trusted by all members of both Houses of Congress and by the American people. That great and patriotic American was Henry Cabot Lodge — not the phony of today who called himself Henry Cabot Lodge Jr. until he was exposed. Lodge completely unmasked Wilson and kept the United States out of the League of Nations.

THE REAL REASON FOR THE LEAGUE OF NATIONS

Here it be comes of great interest to know the real reason for the Wilson, League of Nations plot. As we previously stated, Schiff was sent to the United States to carry out four specific assignments. He was to: — (1) acquire complete control of the U.S. money system; (2) find the right kind of men to serve as stooges for the Great Conspiracy and promote them into the highest offices in our federal government, our Congress, our U.S. Supreme Court, and all federal agencies, such as the State Department, the Pentagon, the Treasury Department, etc.; (3) destroy the unity of the American people by creating minority group strife throughout the nation, especially between the Whites and Blacks as outlined in Israel Cohen's book; and (4) create a movement to destroy religion in the United States with Christianity to be its chief target or victim.

In addition, he was strongly reminded of the imperative directive in the Illuminati blueprint to achieve full control of all mass communications media to be used to brainwash the people into believing and accepting all of the maneuverings of the Great Conspiracy. Schiff was warned that only control of the press — at that time our only mass communications media — would enable him to destroy the unity of the American people.

So Schiff and his co-conspirators set up the National Association for the Advancement of the Colored People (NAACP) in 1909, and the Anti-Defamation League of the B'nai Brith (ADL) in 1913 — both to create the necessary strife. But in the early years, the ADL operated very timidly, perhaps for fear of a pogrom like action by an aroused and engaged American people, and the NAACP was practically dormant because the White leadership didn't realize they would have to develop firebrand Negro leaders, such as Martin Luther King, to spark the then apparently contented mass of Negroes. In addition, he, Schiff, was busy developing and infiltrating the stooges to serve in all high places in our Washington government — and in the job of acquiring control of our money system, and the creation of the 16th Amendment. He also was very busy with organizing the plot for the takeover of Russia. In short, he was kept so busy with all those jobs, that he completely overlooked the supreme job of acquiring complete control of our mass communications media.

That oversight was a direct cause for Wilson's failure to lure the United States into the League of Nations, because when Wilson decided to go to the people to overcome the opposition of the Lodge controlled Senate, despite his established but phony reputation as a great humanitarian, he found himself faced by a solidly united people and by a loyal press whose only ideology was Americanism and the American way of life. Due to the ineptness and ineffectiveness of the ADL and the NAACP, there were no organized minority groups, no Negro problems, no so-called anti-Semitic problems to sway the peoples' thinking. There were no "lefts" and there were no "rights", no prejudices for crafty exploitations. Thus, Wilson's League of Nations appeal fell on deaf ears. And that was the end of Woodrow Wilson, the conspirator's great humanitarian. He quickly abandoned his crusade and returned to Washington, where he shortly died, an imbecile brought on by syphilis, — and that was the end of the League of Nations as a corridor into One World Government.

"IF AT FIRST YOU DON'T SUCCEED, TRY, AGAIN"

That debacle, of course, was a terrible disappointment to the masterminds of the Illuminati Conspiracy, but they were not discouraged. As we have previously stressed, this enemy never quits — they simply reorganize and try from scratch again.

By this time Schiff was very old and slow. He knew it, he knew that the Conspiracy needed a new younger and more active generalship, so on his orders, Colonel House and Bernard Baruch organized and set up what they called the Council on Foreign Relations (CFR), the new name under which the Illuminati would continue to function in the United States. The hierarchy, officers and directors of the CFR are composed principally of descendants of the original Illuminati, many of whom had abandoned their old family names and acquired new Americanized names. For one example, we have Dillon, who was Secretary of Treasury of the United States, whose original name was Lipowski; another example is Paley, head of the CBS TV channel whose true name is Palynski.

The membership of the CFR is approximately 3,000 in number and contained the heads of virtually every industrial empire in America, such as the President of U.S. Steel; Rockefeller, king of the oil industry; Henry Ford, etc. and, of course, all the international bankers. Also, the heads of the tax-free foundations are officers and/or active CFR members. In short, all the men who provide the money and the influence to elect the CFR-chosen Presidents of the United States, the Congressmen, Senators, and those who decide the appointments of our various Secretaries of State, of the Treasury, and of every important federal agency — are members of the CFR, and very obedient members indeed.

Now, just to cement that fact, we will mention the names of a few of the United States presidents who were members of the

CFR: Franklin Roosevelt, Herbert Hoover, Dwight D. Eisenhower, and Jack Kennedy. Others who were considered for the presidency were Thomas E. Dewey, Adlai Stevenson, Richard Nixon, and vice president of the CFR subsidiary, Barry Goldwater. Among the important Cabinet members of the various administrations at one time were: John Foster Dulles, Allen Dulles, Cordele Hull, John J. McLeod, Clarence Dillon, Dean Rusk, Robert McNamara, and, just to emphasize the color of the CFR, we had as members such men as Alger Hiss, Ralph Bunche, Pasvolski, Harry Dexter White, Rudlemane Weiss, Olin Latermore, Philip Jaffe, etc. etc. At the same time, they were flooding thousands of homosexuals and other blackmailable characters into all the federal agencies — from the White House on down. Remember Lyndon Johnson's great friend Jenkins, and Bobby Baker?

ACCOMPLISHMENTS OF THE CFR

Now, there were many jobs the new CFR had to accomplish. They acquired much help, so the first job was to set up various subsidiaries to which they assigned special objectives. We can't name all the subsidiaries in this thesis, but the following are a few: — The Foreign Policy Association (FPA), the World Affairs Council (WAC), the Business Advisory Council (BAC), the notorious ADA (Americans for Democratic Action), the notorious thirteen in Chicago; Barry Goldwater was, and no doubt still is, a vice president of one of the CFR subsidiaries. In addition, the CFR set up special committees in every state in the union to whom they assigned the various local state operations.

Simultaneously, the Rothschilds set up similar CFR like control groups in England, France, Germany and other nations to control world conditions and cooperate with the CFR to bring about another world war. But, the CFR's first and foremost job was to get complete control of our mass communications media. The control of the press was assigned to Rockefeller. Thus, the late Henry Luce, was financed to set up a number of national magazines, among them *LIFE, TIME, FORTUNE* and others which publish in America. The Rockefellers also directly or indirectly financed the Cowell brothers' *LOOK* magazine and a chain of newspapers. They also financed a man named Sam Newhouse to buy up and build a chain of newspapers all over the country, and the late Eugene Meyer, one of the founders of the CFR, bought the *WASHINGTON POST, NEWSWEEK* and other publications. At the same time, the CFR began to develop and nurture a new breed of scurrilous columnists and editorial writers, such as Walter Lippman, Drew Pearson, the Alsops, Herbert Matthews, Erwin Canham, and others of that ilk who called themselves "liberals", who proclaimed that Americanism is isolationism, that isolationism is warmongerism, that anti-Communism is anti-Semitism and racism.

All that took time, of course, but today our entire press, except for some local small town papers and weeklies published by patriotic organizations, is completely controlled by CFR stooges and thus they finally succeeded in breaking America up into a nation of quarreling, wrangling, squabbling, hating factions. Now if you still wonder about the slanted news and outright lies you read in your paper, you have the answer.

To the Lehmans, Goldman, Sachs, Kuhn, Loebs, and the Warburgs, the CFR assigned the job of getting control of the motion picture industry, Hollywood, radio and television; in this they succeeded. If you still wonder about the strange propaganda broadcasts by Ed Murrow, Chet Huntley, Howard K. Smith, Eric Severeid, Drew Pearson, and others of that ilk, you have the answer. If you wonder about all the smut, sex, pornography, and mixed marriage, or single parent films you see on your TV set, all of which is demoralizing our youth, you have the answer.

The whole story of the CFR conspiracy takeover of our mass communications media is far too long to include in this thesis, but you can see how the press, the movies, TV and radio have been, and still are used to brainwash the people and to demoralize our youth, and they have been, and still are encouraging and creating sympathy for rioting Negro civil rights lawlessness.

TO REFRESH MEMORY LET'S GO BACK A BIT

Wilson's flop torpedoed all chances of transforming that League of Nations into the conspirators' hoped for One World Government, so the Jacob Schiff plot had to be done all over again and they organized the CFR to do it. We also know how successfully the CFR did that job of brainwashing and destroying the unity of the American people, but as was the case with the Schiff plot, the climax and the creation of a new housing for their One World Government required another world war, a war that would be even more horrible and more devastating than the First World War in order to get the people of the world to begin clamoring for peace and the means to end all wars. But, the CFR realized that the aftermath of World War II would have to be more carefully planned so that there would be no escape from the new One World Trap — another League of Nations that would emerge from the new war, the trap we now have as the United Nations — and they hit upon a perfect strategy to ensure that there would be no escape.

WORKING TO FORM THE UNITED NATIONS

In 1943, in the midst of the war, they prepared the framework for the United Nations and it was handed over to Roosevelt and our State Department to be given birth by Alger Hiss, Pasvolski, Dalton, Krumble, and other American traitors, thus making the whole scheme a United States baby. Then, to fix our parenthood, New York City was to become the nursery for the monster. After that we could hardly walk out on our own baby, now could we? Anyway, that is how the conspirators figured it would work and so far it has, and the liberal Rockefeller donated land for the United Nations building.

The United Nations Charter was written by Alger Hiss, Pasvolski, Dalton, Krumble and other CFR stooges. A phony so-called conference was then set up in San Francisco in 1945. All the so-called representatives of 50 odd nations gathered there and promptly signed the Charter, and the despicable traitor, Alger Hiss, flew to Washington with it and elatedly submitted it to our Senate, and the Senate — elected by our people to safeguard our security — signed the Charter without so much as reading it. The question remains, how many of our senators were even then traitorous stooges of the CFR? Anyway, it was thus that the people accepted the United Nations as a holy of holies, and enabled traitor, Earl Warren, to virtually destroy our Constitution by basing all his traitorous decisions on the U.N. Charter, thus making the Charter virtually the law of our land.

However, for all the dirty work that would have to be done to solidify the U.N. — the new housing of the One World Plot — they still required the aid of our leaders in Washington. So now we will emphasize the fiendish cleverness of the CFR masterminds.

AMERICAN FOREIGN POLICY: AN ENIGMA?

To the vast majority of the American people, our foreign policy for many years has been a complete enigma. Most of us simply can't understand why this great nation is seemingly floundering so helplessly in the art of diplomacy. We can't understand why our leaders are seemingly so confused and bewildered in all their dealings with Moscow, France, and other nations and with the U.N. We always hear the proclaiming that, in view of our overwhelming economic and military superiority, we must always lead from strength, yet at all summit meetings and conferences, they cringe and stammer and stutter, so to speak, and come out with their tails between their legs.

We couldn't understand the foreign aid to Tito – an avowed enemy; to Poland – an avowed enemy; to all the avowed Communist nations. We can't understand why the expenditure of hundreds of billions of dollars has failed to slow down, let alone stop, the march of Comm-UN-ism. We are perplexed at the seeming ineptness of the State Department, the Defense Department, the CIA, the USIA, of all our federal agencies. Again and again and again, we have been startled, shocked, bewildered, and horrified by their mistakes in Berlin, in Korea, in Laos, in Katanga, in Cuba, in Viet Nam, in the Gulf, in Cosovo — mistakes that always favor the enemy, never the United States. Under the law of averages, they should have made at least one or two mistakes in our favor, but they never do. What's the answer? The answer is the CFR and the parts played by the subsidiaries and stooges in Washington.

Thus, we know that complete control of our foreign relations policy is the key to the success of the entire Illuminati One World Plot. Here is further proof. Earlier we established that Schiff and his gang had financed the Lenin/Trotsky/Stalin takeover of Russia and fashioned its Communist regime into becoming its key instrument to keep the world in turmoil and to finally terrorize all of us into seeking peace in a U.N. One World Government.

But, the conspirators knew that the Moscow gang could not become such an instrument until and unless the whole world would accept the Communist regime as the legitimate de jeur government of Russia. Only one thing could accomplish that — recognition by the United States. The conspirators figured that the whole world would follow our lead and that's when the Wilson flop very nearly wrecked the entire plot.

Throughout the following three Republican administrations, the CFR pulled every trick in their bag to induce Harding, Coolidge and Hoover to grant that recognition, but all three refused. As a result, in the late 1920s, the Stalin regime was in dire straits. Despite all the purges and secret police controls, the Russian people were growing more and more restive. It is a matter of record, admitted by Lipinoff, that during 1930 and 1932, Stalin and his whole gang were always packed and ready for instant flight.

ROOSEVELT TO THE "RESCUE"

Then, in November 1932, the conspirators achieved their greatest coup — they landed Franklin Roosevelt in the White House — crafty, unscrupulous, utterly without conscience, that charlatan traitor turned the tide for them. Without even asking consent of Congress, he unlawfully proclaimed recognition for the Stalin regime. That did it and exactly as the conspirators figured, the whole world did follow our lead. Automatically, that squelched the previously growing resistance movement of the Russian people. That automatically launched the greatest menace the civilized world has ever known. The rest is too well known to need repeating.

We know how Roosevelt and his traitorous State Department kept building up the Communist menace right here in our own country and thus throughout the world. We know how he perpetrated the Pearl Harbor atrocity for his excuse to hurl us into World War II. We know all about his secret meetings with Stalin at Yalta and how he, with Eisenhower's crafty help, delivered the Balkans and Berlin to Moscow, and last, but not least, we know that that 20th century traitor not only dragged us into that new corridor, the United Nations — into One World Government — but actually schemed all the arrangements to plant it within our country. In short, the day that Roosevelt entered the White House, the CFR conspirators regained full control of our foreign relations machinery, and firmly established the United Nations as the housing for the Illuminati One World Government.

ANOTHER CRISIS IN THE MAKING

We wish to stress one other vital point. That Wilson, League of Nations plot brought Schiff and his gang to the realization that control of just the Democratic Party was not enough. True, they could create a crisis during the Republican administration, as they did in 1929 with their Federal Reserve manufactured crash and Great Depression, which would bring another Democrat stooge back into the White House. But they realized that a four-year disruption in their control of our And here is another grizzly detail about those concentration camps — many of the Hitler soldier executioners in those camps had previously been sent to Russia to acquire their arts of torture and brutalization in order to emphasize the horrors of these atrocities. All this created a new worldwide hatred for the Germany people, but it still didn't provide a cause for war; thereupon, Hitler was incited to demand the Sudetenland. You remember how Chamberlain and the then diplomats of Czechoslovak and France surrendered to that demand? That led for further Hitlerian demands for territories in Poland and then the French Soir territories. Those demands were rejected. Then came his pact with Stalin. Hitler had been screaming hatred against Communism — oh, how he ranted against Communism — but actually Nazism was nothing but Socialism, and Communism is in fact Socialism. But, Hitler disregarded all that. He entered into a pact with Stalin to attack and divide Poland between them. While Stalin marched into one part of Poland, for which he was never blamed, the Illuminati masterminds saw to that, Hitler launched a blitzkrieg on Poland from his side. The conspirators finally had their new World War and what a horrible war it was.

THE UNITED NATIONS IS ACHIEVED AT LAST

In 1945, the conspirators finally achieved the United Nations — their new housing for their One World Government, and truly amazing, all of the American people hailed this foul outfit as a holy of holies. Even after all the true facts about how the U.N. was created were revealed, the American people continued to worship that evil outfit. Even after Alger Hiss was unmasked as a Soviet spy and traitor, the American people continued to believe in the U.N. Even after it was publicly revealed that the secret agreement between Hiss and Malakoff — that a Russian would always be the head of the Military Secretariat, and by that token, the real master of the U.N. — most of the American people continued to believe that the U.N. could do no wrong. Even after Trigmon Li, the first Secretary General of the U.N., confirmed his Molotov secret agreement in his book, *For The Cause Of Peace,* the vast majority of our people refused to lose faith in the U.N. Even after the truth about the Korean War was revealed, how the Russian General Basiliev — head of that U.N. Military Secretariat — was given a leave of absence by the U.N. so that he could take command of the North Koreans and Red Chinese, who were fighting the so-called U.N. police action under our own General Macarthur, who by orders of the U.N. was fired by Truman in order to prevent his winning that war. Our people still believed in that U.N. despite our thousands of sons who were murdered and maimed in that war. The people continued to regard the U.N. as a world means for peace; even after it was revealed in 1951 that the U.N. — using our own American soldiers under U.N. command and the U.N. flag, in collusion with our traitorous State Department and the Pentagon — had been invading many small cities in California and Texas in order to perfect their plan for the complete takeover of our country. Most of our people brushed it off and continued their belief that the U.N. is a holy of holies.

UNITED NATIONS' DECEIT

Did you know that the U.N. Charter was written by traitor Alger Hiss, Molotov and Vischinski? That Hiss and Molotov had made that secret agreement that the Military Chief of the U.N. was always to be a Russian appointed by Moscow? Did you know that at their secret meetings at Yalta, Roosevelt and Stalin, at the behest of the Illuminati operating as the CFR, decided that the U.N. must be placed on American soil. Did you know that most of the U.N. Charter was copied intact, word for word, from Marx' Communist Manifesto and Russia's so-called Constitution? Did you know that the only two Senators who voted against the U.N. so-called treaty were the only two Senators who had read it? Did you know that since the U.N. was founded Communist enslavement has grown from 250 million to way more than one billion? Did you know that since the U.N. was founded to ensure peace, there have been more than 20 major wars incited by the U.N. — just as they have now incited the war against little Cosovo? Did you know that under the U.N. setup, the American taxpayers have been forced to make up U.N. treasury deficits of many millions of dollars because of Russia's refusal or inability to pay her share? Did you know that the U.N. has never passed a resolution condemning Russia or her so-called satellites, but always condemns our allies? Did you know that J. Edgar Hoover said the overwhelming majority of the Communist delegations to the U.N. are espionage agents?

And, 66 senators voted for a Consular Treaty to open our entire country to Russian spies and saboteurs. Did you know that the U.N. helps Russia's conquest of the world by preventing the free world from taking any action whatsoever except to debate each new aggression in the U.N. General Assembly? Did you know that at the time of the Korean War there were 60 Nations in the U.N., yet 95% of the U.N. forces were our American sons, and practically 100% of the cost was paid by the United States taxpayers?

And, surely you know that the U.N. policy during the Korean War was to prevent us from winning that war. Did you know that all those battle plans of General MacArthur had to go first to the U.N. to be relayed to Basiliev — Commander of the North Koreans and Red Chinese — and that any future wars fought by our sons under the U.N. flag would have to be fought under the control of the U.N. Security Council? Did you know that the U.N. has never done anything about the 80,000 Russian-Mongolian troops that occupied Hungary? Where was the U.N. when the Hungarian freedom fighters were slaughtered by the Russians? Did you know that the U.N. and its peace army turned the Congo over to the Communists? Did you know that the U.N.'s own so-called peace force was used to crush, rape, and kill the white anti-Communists in Katanga? Did you know that the U.N. stood by and did nothing while Red China invaded Laos and Viet Nam — that it did nothing when Nehru invaded Gore and other Portuguese territories? Did you know that the U.N. was directly responsible for aiding Castro? That the U.N. does absolutely nothing about the many thousands of Cuban youngsters who are shipped to Russia for Communist indoctrination? Did you know that Adlai Stevenson, of all people, said the free world must expect to lose more and more decisions in the U.N.? Did you know that the U.N. openly proclaims that its chief objective is One World Government, which means One World Laws, One World Court, One World Army, One World Navy, One World Air Force, One World Schools, and a One World Church in which Christianity would be prohibited? Did you know that a U.N. law has been passed to disarm all American citizens and to transfer all our Armed Forces to the U.N.? Such a law was secretly signed by "Saint" Jack Kennedy in 1961. Do you realize how that fits in with Article 47, paragraph 3, of the U.N. Charter, which states, *"The military staff committee of the U.N. shall be responsible through the Security Council for the strategic direction of all armed forces placed at the disposal of the Security Council."?*

And, when our Armed Forces are transferred to the U.N., our sons will be forced to serve and die under U.N. command all over the world. This will happen unless we fight to get the U.N. out of the U.S.

SOME MEN WOULD LIKE TO FIX WHAT'S WRONG

Did you know that Congressman Ron Paul has submitted a bill to get the U.S. out of the U.N. — the "American Sovereignty Restoration Act" (H.R. 1146) to "terminate all participation by the United States in the United Nations, and any organ, specialized agency, commission, or other formally affiliate body of the United Nations"? Well, he has. Not only are "reforms" not the answer, but reforming the U.N. by, for example, making it less bureaucratic could actually serve as a pretext for giving the U.N. more power.

So many patriotic Americans all over the country are writing to their representatives to support H.R. 1146. The address for any member of the House of Representatives is: — House Office Building, Washington, D.C. 20515.

OTHER ORGANIZATIONS ARE INVOLVED

Now, did you know that the National Council of Churches passed a resolution in San Francisco which states that the United States will have to subordinate its will to that of the United Nations, and that all American citizens must be prepared to accept it? Is your church a member of the National Council of Churches? In connection with that, bear in mind that God is never mentioned in the United Nations Charter, and their meetings are never opened with prayer. The creators of the U.N. stipulated in advance that there should be no mention of God or of Jesus Christ in the U.N. Charter or in its U.N. headquarters. Does your pastor subscribe to that? Find out. Furthermore, do you know that the great majority of so-called nations in the U.N. are anti-Christianity? That the U.N. is a completely God-less organization by order of its creators — the Illuminati CFR?

Now, have you heard enough of the truth about the Illuminati's United Nations? Do you want to leave your sons and our precious country to the unholy mercy of the Illuminati's United Nations Command? If you don't, write, telegraph, phone, or email your Representatives and Senators that they must support Congressman Paul's bill to get the U.S. out of the U.N., and the U.N. out of the U.S. Do it today — now — before you forget. It is the only salvation for your sons and for our country.

THE DESTRUCTION OF RELIGION IN THE U.S.A.

Now, we have one more vital message to deliver. As we mentioned before, one of the four specific assignments Rothschild gave Jacob Schiff was to create a movement to destroy religion in the United States with Christianity to be its chief target. For very obvious reasons, the Anti-Defamation League wouldn't dare to attempt it because such an attempt could create the most terrible bloodbath in the history of the world, not only for the ADL and conspirators, but for millions of innocent Jews. So Schiff turned that job over to Rockefeller for another specific reason — the destruction of Christianity could be accomplished only by those who are entrusted to preserve it — by the pastors: the men of the cloth.

To start, John D. Rockefeller picked up a young so-called "Christian" minister by the name of Dr. Harry F. Ward — "Reverend" Ward if you please. At that time he was teaching religion at the Union Theological Seminary. Rockefeller found a very willing Judas in this Reverend. Thereupon, in 1907, he financed him to set up the Methodist Foundation of Social Service and Ward's job was to teach bright young men to become so-called "ministers of Christ" and to place them as pastors of churches. While teaching them to become ministers, the Reverend Ward also taught them how to very subtly and craftily preach to their congregations that the entire story of Christ is a myth, to cast doubts on the divinity of Christ, to cast doubts about the Virgin Mary, in short — to cast doubts on Christianity as a whole.

It was not to be a direct attack, but much of it by crafty insinuation that was to be applied particularly to the youth in the Sunday Schools. Remember Lenin's statement, *"Give me just one generation of youth and I'll transform the whole world."*

Then, in 1908, the Methodist Foundation of Social Service, which incidentally was America's first Communist front organization, changed its name to the Federal Council of Churches. By 1950, the Federal Council of Churches was becoming very suspect, so in 1950, they changed the name to the National Council of Churches. Do we have to tell you more about how this National Council of Churches is deliberately destroying faith in Christianity? We don't think so, but this we will say. If you are a member of any congregation whose pastor and church are members of this Judas organization, you, and your contributions are helping the Illuminati's plot to destroy religion, and your faith in God and Jesus Christ. Thus, you are deliberately delivering your children to be indoctrinated with this belief in God and Church which can easily transform them into atheists. Find out immediately if your church is a member of the National Council of Churches and, for the love of God and your children and "grans", if it is, withdraw from it at once. However, let us warn you, that same destroying religious process has been infiltrated into almost all other denominations.

If you have seen the Negro march on Selma and other such demonstrations, you have seen how the Negro mobs are led and encouraged by ministers and even Catholic priests and nuns who march along with them. As a matter of fact, the Mormon Church is about the only one we know of that is clean of that kind of Judas infiltration, but of course there are also many individual churches and pastors who are honest and sincere. Find one such for yourself and for your children. Incidentally, this same Rev. Harry F. Ward was also one of the founders of the American Civil Liberties Union, a notorious pro-Communist organization. He was the actual head of it from 1920-1940. He also was a co-founder of the American League Against War and Fascism, which under a Mr. Broder became the Communist Party of the United States. In short, Ward's entire background reeks of Communism, and he was identified as a member of the Communist Party. He died a vicious traitor to both his church and his country and this was the man old John D. Rockefeller picked and financed to destroy America's Christian religion in accordance with the orders given to Schiff by the Rothschilds.

IN CONCLUSION WE HAVE THIS TO SAY

You probably are familiar with the story of how one Dr. Frankenstein created a monster to do his will of destroying his chosen victims, but how, instead in the end that monster turned on his own creator, Frankenstein, and destroyed him. Well, the

Illuminati CFR, has created a monster called the United Nations, who — supported by their minority groups, rioting Negroes, the traitorous mass communications media, and the traitors in Washington — was created to destroy the American people. Well, you now know a lot about that many-headed hydra monster. You now know the names of those who created that monster. You now know all their names, and we predict that one fine day the American people will come fully awake and cause that very monster to destroy its creators and itself.

It is really true that the majority of our people are being brainwashed, deceived, and deluded by the traitorous press, TV and radio, and by our traitors in Washington, but surely, by now, enough is known about the United Nations to mark that outfit as a deadly rattlesnake in our midst. Our only wonder is, what it will take to awaken and arouse our people to action regarding the full truth.

The Trilateral Commission was established in 1973, by David Rockefeller because the Council on Foreign Relations was gaining such a bad reputation. It was this same Trilateral Commission that selected an unknown peanut farmer, completely ignorant of world affairs, and made him Governor of Georgia. Still unknown outside of Georgia, they spent untold millions on the greatest media blitzkrieg this country has ever seen, to make this man President of the United States. His closest advisors and important appointments were usually Trilateral members.

The great controversy of the battle of evil with good is originally explained in allegorical terms in the Judeo-Christian Bible where it speaks of God, the angels and his two sons, Jesus and Lucifer. Lucifer hid the light within himself, and Jesus shined it forth for all mankind declaring, "Ye shall know the truth and the truth shall make you free." — John 8:32.

Chapter 8
Money? Or Mammon?
by David Daniels

"Permit me to issue and control the money of a nation and I care not who makes its laws." — Mayer Rothchild, International Banker

We become familiar with money at an early age. Young children are taught how to count and handle money. We use money so frequently that we take it for granted, but do we really understand what it is?

Money is spoken of in the Bible by weight. Biblical law specifically commands that financial transactions be made in terms of honest measurements of weight. God is plain spoken on this subject in Leviticus:

"Ye shall do no unrighteousness in judgement, in meteyard, in weight, or in measure. Just balances, just weights, a just ephah, and just hin, shall ye have: I am the Lord your God, which brought you out of the land of Egypt." Therefore shall ye observe all my statutes, and all my judgments, and do them: I am the Lord." — Leviticas 19:35-37

Historically and biblically, gold and silver have served as money. We should remember that money, in its true form, is a **commodity**. Money is not a measurement of value or wealth, as most people have been falsely taught to believe.

Dishonest governments hate this fact because if they can't convince the people that they control the money, they can't control the people. This is the reason why governments deceive the people into believing that they supply and regulate the currency. The international bankers who our government allows to supply our currency create as much money as they need. God's Law forbids this:

"A false balance is abomination to the Lord: but a just weight is his delight. Delight is not seemly for a fool; much less for a servant to have rule over princes." - Proverbs 11:1, 20:10, 23.

The prophets also warn that: *"Thy silver is become dross, thy wine mixed with water. When will the new moon be gone, that we may sell corn? and the sabbath, that we may set forth wheat, making the ephah small, and the shekel great, and falsifying the balances by deceit? That we may buy the poor for silver, and the needy for a pair of shoes; yea, and sell the refuse of the wheat? Are there yet the treasures of wickedness in the house of the wicked, and the scant measure that is abominable? Shall I count them pure with the wicked balances, and with the bag of deceitful weights? For the rich thereof are full of violence, and the inhabitants thereof have spoken lies, and their tongue is deceitful in their mouth. Therefore will I make thee sick in smiting thee . . . because of thy sin."* - Isaiah 1:22; Amos 8:5,6; Micah 6:10-13.

This type of counterfeiting is a dishonest increase in the supply of money. The Bible condemns counterfeiting whether its done by individuals, governments, or international bankers. Inflating the currency is theft.

    Money is not simply worthless paper without any gold or silver backing anymore. It can be nothing more than electronic blips sent from computer to computer. Inflation can speed right along with nothing to stop it. The government in Washington D.C. (District of Criminals) spends the money that it steals from the taxpayers on projects that are biblically forbidden; and the beneficiaries of inflation (debtors and people who receive government checks) complain about higher prices as they spend the dollars stolen from productive citizens. The willful government policy of inflation, along with the greed and covetousness of the citizens, causes poverty and unemployment.

The lunatic fringe liberals of the political left think that the government should pay for their socialist programs. How do they think that government pays for anything? There are only two ways, taxation and inflation. So what the liberals really want is for the productive citizens to pay the costs for their programs — not voluntarily, but by being plundered.

The Bible does allow for government taxation, but not much. What Scripture teaches is that the rate of taxation determines the size of the state. Anything higher than 10% is an attempt by rulers to be like God, extracting a tithe. Interventionist and socialist programs are not biblical. Why should we expect God to sustain us as a nation if we as Christians don't obey his Word?

"The paper money disease has been a pleasant habit thus far and will not be dropped voluntarily anymore than an addict will, without a struggle, give up dope." - The late Congressman Howard Buffet, 1948

Have you ever had to borrow money? If you don't belong to one of the truly elite families in this country that's probably a silly question. All of us working class people have had to borrow money for homes, automobiles, education, etc., but did you realize that what you were borrowing and working so hard for to pay back had absolutely no real value? Let me explain.

Before 1933 a dollar bill couldn't be spent. People accepted them in place of real money because they did represent real money, silver or gold coins minted by the United States Mint, not the non-federal Federal Reserve. It meant that the United States owed you real money (silver or gold) in exchange for your dollar bills. Now what we have is Federal Reserve Notes that are backed by nothing at all, and a fractional reserve banking system that intentionally creates inflation.

The non-federal Federal Reserve allows banks to keep a small percentage of deposits on hand and loan out the rest at interest. Technically, banks are always bankrupt. They never have enough money on hand to cover demand deposit withdrawals if lots of people wanted their money all at the same time.

Here's where it begins to look like a the real racket that it is. Banks can use their loans as bank assets. They simply enter the loan to you in a ledger or in the computer as a deposit to the account of you, the borrower. This trick allows the bank to handle it according to the banking "rules" on deposits.

A bank is required to keep on hand only 16% of demand deposits as a reserve. So, if a customer deposits $1,000.00, the bank can loan out $840.00 of it to another customer ($1,000.00 minus 16% kept on reserve). When the bank loans that next customer the $840.00, they record this as a deposit to that customer's account. Now they record 16% of this loan as a reserve and loan out the remaining $700.00 to another customer. The $700.00 dollars is recorded as a deposit, 16% recorded as kept on reserve, and another $575.00 loan can then be made. They can repeat this until the amount loanable reaches $1.00. From that original $1,000.00 deposit, the bank makes $6,000.00 in loans bearing interest at whatever the going rate happens to be at the time.

Now you can see how banks really make their money — off bank "assets" that really do not exist. Banks are running this scam on us and they want to make us feel like they're doing us a huge favor when they loan us this so-called money at way too high percentages of interest. The profits that they make is only part of the story. The thing that's really killing us is the increase of credit to the money supply of the economy. That is the *sole* cause of inflation.

Chapter 9
America? A Conquered Land?

"To achieve World Government, it is necessary to remove from the minds of man, their individualism, their loyalty of family traditions, their national patriotism, and their religious dogmas." — Brock Chisolm, Director of the U.N. World Health Organization

AN ECONOMIC CONQUEST is taking place wherein our nation is being placed under 'tribute' to a foreign entity without the use of visual force. Americans do not realize that we're being conquered and are under siege.

This conquest began when our conquerors gained control of the monetary system of our nation in 1913 and this led in the following years to World War I. This foreign influence does not want to arouse our suspicions so they made and are making slow and gradual changes in our system of government, to their benefit. They are slowly usurping the financial assets of our nation. Tribute is being payed to them in the form of unconstitutional 'legal' debts and taxes which we are led to believe are for our own good and the good of others to protect us from an imaginary 'enemy'. Tribute is also being paid to them in the form of engineered inflation. This 'enemy' has supposedly become our 'benefactor' and 'protector'.

Although this method is slower than outright military conquest, it is longer lasting because we do not see a military force being used against us. We are free to participate in the elections of our rulers but the outcomes are manipulated by those in control. Without realizing it our nation is under siege. Our wealth is being gradually transferred to our captors and our conquest is nearly complete.

Our economic problems are not the result of mis-management. They are being deliberately engineered by self-serving money-powers who have for almost a century played an integral role in a deliberate, silent, weaponless war against "we the people" and our property. Their silent weapons are **seduction** through gradual changes, **manipulations** by fear, words of art, and deceptive syntax. Their assault is on private ownership. And their goal is to slowly undermine the Constitution of our fair land, usurp the Rights of the People, take away our Sovereignty, immobilize our middle class, and seize our property and capital under the semblance and color of law within the pretext of government. Their mission is to peaceably reduce America to a "world state" within a global, international, One World, socialist-democratic Government under their economic control and United Nations (U.N.) rule. Under the guise of so-called 'peace', the U.N. was created by the Council of Foreign Relations (CFR.).

In 1987, 81% of the United Nations delegation voted with the socialistic nations of the world. Only 19% voted with the United States of America. The bureaucracy of the U.N. still opposes free enterprise in favor of governmental planning and socialism. A 1991 report states that the U.N. Development Program spends $1.5 billion a year **"helping authoritarian governments preserve the status quo."** A prevailing government under a globalist U.N. rule would be — not republican as in America today — but authoritarian. The unique and fundamentally American ideals of sovereignty, property rights, privacy, free enterprise, the right to control our children, and a nation under God, are completely contradictory to the socialistic principles of the One World Plan — and these ideals are now under siege.

Under the American Constitution, the *people* are sovereign. Under Socialism, the *government* is sovereign. Constitutional citizens are free. Socialistic citizens are subjects. Our Constitution *protects* property rights. Socialism *abolishes* property rights. Our Constitution protects *free enterprise.* Socialism protects **government monopolies.** Our Constitution demands monetary creation for and by the People through Congress (but this demand has NEVER been obeyed!). Socialism demands Central Banks and world economic control. Our Constitution demands equally apportioned direct taxes (but this demand has NEVER been obeyed!). Socialism demands graduated direct taxes. Our Constitution demands **Due Process of Law.** Socialism demands **Pre-Judgement Liens.** Our Constitution demands **Freedom of the Press** (the media). Socialism demands **government controlled media.** Our Constitution demands **Freedom of Speech.** Socialism demands **the implementation of "Gag" Orders.** Our Constitution demands **the Common Law of Justice, Reason, and Truth.** Socialism demands **Legislative Absolutism.** Our Constitution protects **Freedom of Religion and a God based society.** Socialism protects **the prohibition of a belief in God.**

The main purpose of the Council on Foreign Relations (CFR) which created the United Nations, is to promote disarmament, the end of United States sovereignty and national independence, and the submergence of the United States into an all-powerful, One World Government. This is the only objective revealed to 95% of the more than one thousand U.N. members. There are two other ulterior purposes that the CFR influence is being used to promote, but it is unlikely that they are known to more than 75 or so members. These two purposes have never been identified in writing — 1) world control and 2) the socialization of the advanced nations of the world. To achieve these objectives, those seeking power must make America socialistically 'compatible' by weakening our national sovereignty and financially immobilizing our middle class through job losses (exported to other nations) and seizures of American property.

The philosophy of socialism is that the *bourgeoisie* (the middle class) is the *enemy* of socialism and must be stripped of their wealth. Karl Marx stated that a gradual income tax was necessary *"to crush the middle class under the guise of a need to finance the government."* This would return those in power to the static society of the middle ages where everyone is either a peasant or a prince. The unconstitutional graduated income tax — combined with managed inflation — moves the middle class into higher and higher income tax brackets through cost of living raises, but these raises do not compensate for the additional taxes paid because of such a raise. This, combined with fewer deductions available to the middle class each year, transfers a continuously larger portion of middle class property to the government.

Karl Marx came up with the concept of a **"weaponless war"**.

In 1872, speaking in Amsterdam, Marx stated, *"a social revolution or economic conquest can be accomplished by peaceful means in America by taking advantage of libertarian traditions and free institutions, to subvert them."*

The concept of a New World Order is as old as the Declaration of Independence.

On May 1, 1776 (May day is still considered by many to be the most important holiday), a German professor of canon law at Ingolstadt, Germany, Adam Weishaupt, organized a secret society which he called Perfektibilisten, but which later took on the old name of Illuminati. Its ex-Jesuit founder — following the model of the *Society of Jesus* — divided its associates into grades of initiation, and pledged them to obey their leaders in a campaign to "unite all men capable of independent thought" to make man "a masterpiece of reason and thus to attain the highest perfection in the art of government."

To give their organization credibility, the Illuminati infiltrated the Continental Order of Freemasons, led by the money powers of their generation. The New Order that followed was called the "Illuminated Freemasonry". The philosophies of the Illuminati — which were the basis for the concept of a "New World Order" (Novus Order Seclorum) — were also the fundamental principles upon which Communism and Socialism were built. They included, 1) the elimination of all God based religions, 2) the establishment of a One World Government, 3) the elimination of all other independent governments, 4) the elimination of all national sovereignty, and 5) the nationalization of resource production into the hands of the government. In 1782, the headquarters of Illuminated Freemasonry move to Frankfurt, Germany — an area controlled by the Rothchild family of Europe.

In 1784 the elector of Bavaria, Karl Theodor, outlawed all secret societies, and the Order of the Illuminati suffered an early death — or so history thought and taught. (The Illuminati were key players in the Bolshevik Revolution in Russia).

Weishaupt's greatest disciple was Moses Mordicai Marx Levy, alias Karl Marx. Weishaupt and Marx proposed a long range plan for looting the world and gaining international power. First, they would control the banks and money. Second, they would create a progressive income tax that would be perverted into a capital tax. And third, they would create a confiscatory inheritance tax.

To stop their plan for a New World Order, we must bind the monetary powers by the awesome chains of our American Constitution! The United Nations Charter *cannot* be allowed to take the place of our American Constitution! The Supremacy Clause in our Constitution [Article VI, Section 2] which states, **"This Constitution and the laws of the United States which shall be made in pursuance thereof and all treaties, etc., etc.,"** specifies that such laws and treaties must be made **"in pursuance of the Constitution"** — not contrary to it. The Constitution cannot be in conflict with itself.

Further, Article VI, Section 3 makes it clear that the Supreme Law of the Land referred to in Section 2 is the Constitution. It states, **"The Senators and Representatives before mentioned, and the members of the several state legislatures, and all executive and judicial officers, both of the**

United States and of the several States, shall be bound by oath or affirmation, to support this Constitution..."

It would be ludicrous to conclude that those "bound by oath" to uphold our Constitution, would instead uphold the U.N. Charter in its stead.

The concept that there can be two supreme Laws in one Land, which are contradictory to each other, is absurd and defies reason. The very definition of the word "Supreme" nullifies such an erroneous conclusion. *"Any opinion, however strongly expressed, has no authority beyond the reasoning by which it is supported, and binds no one..."* [*Bouvier's 14th Ed. Law Dictionary,* from 4 Wheat, 402].

Further, the case of *Reid v. Covert,* 354 U.S. 1 (1957) held that, *"no agreement with a foreign nation can confer power on the Congress, or on any other branch of Government, which is free from the restraints of the Constitution."* Also, the Emanuel Law Outlines for Constitutional Law on p.51 states that, *"a treaty may NOT violate any constitutional prohibitions of guarantees."*

Some feel that the globalists will try to take our Constitution away from us through the Federal Emergency Management Act (FEMA), under the guise of a national emergency. However, any such action would be completely unlawful. *"No emergency justifies a violation of any Constitutional provision."* (16 Am, Jur. 2nd Ed. Section 71-72.) The chains of our Constitution cannot be and will not be circumvented!

Insiders state that the total membership of the C.F.R., which is spearheading this un-American "New World Order", is only about 2,500 members. Among those only 500 or so have any power and it is estimated that 12 or less know the full ulterior purposes of the C.F.R. and the United Nations. The rest of the members are well respected members of the academia, media, and business, as well as distinguished governmental and military figure-heads who give the appearance or "credibility" to the organization. That's a very small group against 250 or so million Patriotic Americans! (2/100,000%) (fewer than two individuals for every 100,000 Americans!)

Corrupt legislation and engineered ignorance got America into this financial abyss, and education and good legislation can and will set us free from the control of these foreign monetary vultures! We must wage a fearless, intellectual war with our own silent Godly weapons. Weapons that are more powerful than all of theirs combined! These weapons are the Constitution of these United States, the Higher Laws of Principle, and the Truth that shall set and keep us free!

We must go forward as "sheep among wolves" and as "doves among vultures" — and as a "nation under God"! We must re-educate America, reclaim our God Given Rights, re-assert our Sovereignty and re-claim our America for ourselves and for our posterity, so help us God!

"He has sounded forth the trumpet that shall never call retreat, He is sifting out the hearts of men before His judgment seat; O be swift, my soul, to answer Him, be jubilant, my feet, — Our God is marching on."

— *Julia Ward Howe*

Chapter 10
Restoring America

The Declaration of Independence is out Nation's birth certificate and the cornerstone of our Constitution. Its policies must be pursued in conducting our Nations affairs.

There can only be one "Supreme Law" for any Nation. For the United States, it is the Declaration of Independence (including the Bill of Rights), and all lawfully ratified Amendments. The pros, cons, and full impact were underscored by the voters and their representatives prior to ratification. The purpose was (and is) in pursuance of the principles, procedures, and intent of our Declaration of Independence and the preamble of our Constitution.

Any lawful change to the form, principles, and/or operational procedures of our duly constituted government must be approved by 75% of our state legislatures. None have ratified any major changes. Therefore (to be lawful) any Treaty, Charter, Foreign Constitution, Covenant, Legislative Act, International Convention, etc., must be in pursuance of the spirit and intent of the principles set forth in our Declaration of Independence and the preamble to our Constitution.

The Constitution of the United States is a compact between sovereign and independent states. As its principals and under the Law of Agency, it is they (the states) who posses the ultimate authority and responsibility for its proper interpretation and implementation.

The United States Supreme Court was correct in saying: (a) "This court has regularly and uniformly recognized the supremacy of the Constitution over a treaty." (Reid vs. Covert), (b) "All laws repugnant to the Constitution are null and void." (Marbury vs. Madison), (c) "Where rights secured by the Constitution are involved, there can be no rule making or legislation which could abrogate them." (Miranda vs. Arizona).

Our Constitution's 10th Amendment stating: " the powers not delegated to the United States by the Constitution are reserved to the States respectively, or to the people." Federalist Paper #41 states: "For what purpose could the enumeration of particular powers be inserted if these and all others were meant to be included in the preceding general power?" This provides incontestable evidence that the federal government's only lawful powers are the specific and limited powers set forth in the Constitution.

No Federal Agent has, nor ever had, the lawful authority to dissolve the Constitutional Compact nor distort its intent. "Where Congress exceeds its authority relative to the states, departure from the constitutional plan cannot be ratified by "consent" of state officials." U.S. Supreme Court (N.Y. vs. U.S., 112S. CT. 2408, 1992).

A FIVE POINT PLAN — THESE CHANGES WILL RESTORE THE CONSTITUTION OF THE UNITED STATES AND SAVE AMERICA:

1) Stop further growth of the Federal Government and set up a five year period to phase out all federal departments, bureaus, boards, commissions, and other activities that are outside of the duties assigned to it by the States through the Constitution.

2) Demand that Congress exercise its option to repurchase the Federal Reserve System and return the monetary system to government ownership and control as mandated by the Founder's in Article 1, Section 8, Paragraph 5, of the United States Constitution.

3) The President and Congress, by whatever legal means necessary, must disavow any notion that the United Nations Charter or any other agreement or treaty with any other nation or groups of nations is superior to the United States Constitution in

any matter pertaining to United States citizens, states, territories, and possessions. The Keystone of our foreign policy should be to follow the advice of President Washington and be friends to all nations but make no entangling alliances with any. If this means withdrawing from the United Nations and from treaties with individual nations or groups of nations, so be it. The oath of office taken by the President and the Congress of the United States binds them to act only in the best interest of this nation and its citizens within the powers granted to the Federal Government *by the people* through the Constitution.

4) We the must stop trying to be the World's Policeman and allow every nation and people the same right of self determination that we enjoy ourselves. We must bring our military forces home and keep our National Defense so strong that no one will dare to attack us.

5) The Constitution grants no authority for federal government gifts of American taxpayer's money to rulers and people of other nations. Furthermore, it is not in our best interest to do so This practice must be stopped in all categories. Those people and organizations who want to assist other people are perfectly free to do so with their *own* money. The most successful relief assistance to others in time of disaster is done through private sources instead of governments.

These changes will restore the Constitution and save America from default.

Chapter 11
It's Time For The Solution

Currently all we do is exchange FED money (interest attached) for real U.S. money (interest-free), dollar for dollar, as Kennedy tried to do. We should not be required to pay interest on our own currency. According to Benjamin Franklin, this was one of the primary reasons we fought the Revolutionary War. Today we are still fighting the very same family of bankers.

The U.S. Government can buy back the FED at any time for $450 million (per Congressional record). The U.S. Treasury could then collect all the profit on our money instead of the 300 or so original shareholders of the FED. The $5.5 trillion of U.S. debt could be exchanged dollar for dollar with U.S. non-interest bearing currency when the debt becomes due.

There would be no inflation because there would be no additional currency in circulation. Personal income tax could be cut if we bought back the FED and thereafter the economy would expand. According to the Constitution, Congress is supposed to control the creation of money, keeping the amount of inflation or deflation in check. If Congress isn't doing their job, they should be voted out of office. Unfortunately, voters can't vote the FED or its Chairman out of office.

If the government has a deficit, we could handle it as Lincoln and Kennedy did. Print our own money and circulate it into the economy, but this time interest-free. Today the FED, through foreign banks, owns much of our debt and therefore controls us, politically and civilly. The FED will cease to exist as taxpayers become informed and tell other taxpayers; the news media and Congress will have no choice but to meet the demands of grass roots America.

AMERICA DECEIVED

By law, according to the Congressional record, we can buy back the FED for the original investment of the FED's 300 shareholders, which is $450 million. If each taxpayer paid $25, we could buy back the FED and all the profit would flow into the U.S. Treasury. In other words, by Congress allowing the constitutionally illegal FED to continue, all of your taxes go to the shareholders of the FED and their bankers. Note: The people who enacted the FED started the IRS within months of the FED's inception, in order to finance the anticipated national debt. The FED buys U.S. debt with money it prints from nothing, then charges the U.S. taxpayers interest.

The government created the income tax to pay the interest expense on the national debt, to the FED's shareholders, but the income tax act was never legally passed by Congress. The FED is illegal per Article 1, Section 8 of the United States Constitution. No state legally ratified the 16th Amendment making income tax legal. Currently, fewer and fewer Americans are being convicted for refusal to pay income taxes. In IRS jury trials, the jury, by law, must decide if the law is just. If taxpayers do not believe the law is just, the jury may declare the accused innocent.

Judges are legally bound to inform juries of their right to determine the fairness of a law. Judges often do not disclose this information so they can control the court outcome. Luckily, more and more citizens are becoming informed. If one juror feels the law is unfair, they can find the defendant innocent. In Utah, the IRS quit prosecuting taxpayers because the jurors' verdict is not guilty. Please tell your friends, and sit in the next jury.

If we eliminate the FED and uphold the Constitution, we could balance the budget and eliminate the personal income tax. In Congressional hearings on September 30, 1941, FED Chairman Eccles admitted that the FED creates new money from thin air (printing press money), and loans it back to us at interest.

On June 6, 1960, the FED President, Mr. Allen, essentially admitted the same thing. If you or I did this we would go to jail.

It is time to abolish the FED! Tell your friends the truth and win America back. We don't even need to *buy* back the FED. We only need to print money the way the Constitution requires — not the new proposed international money. We want to keep our national sovereignty and print real U.S. money.

Why has Congress allowed the FED to continue? If a Congressman tries to abolish the FED, the banks fund the Congressperson's opponent in the next election. The new Congressman will obviously support the FED. When Congressmen retire, political campaign funds are not taxed. Get elected and be a millionaire if you vote right. By the way, the profit of the FED is not taxed either.

Once America understands this, and takes action, Congressmen will then gladly abolish the FED. In 1992, Illinois Congressman Crane introduced a bill, co-sponsored by 40 other Congressman, to audit the FED. This is a step in the right direction, but it will not complete the job.

America is a great nation. As "We the People" become informed, the media and Congress will be forced to buy back the FED, balance the budget, significantly cut taxes, and stop allowing bribes to determine voting strategies. Many politicians claim they will change their platform to include abolishing the FED if enough people become informed. **IT IS UP TO YOU TO INFORM THE PEOPLE.**

The FED hopes you will be passive and not act on this information. The Mountain Man believes in grass roots America — we are waking up America. Ultimately, the battle plan is to inform all Americans and demand change in the media and Congress. True Americans should run for office and throw out the politicians who allow this fraud to continue. Congress is afraid to deal with this issue. That's why each person needs to go to their local county and state government with the proper paperwork and ask them to abolish the FED. With the proper documents, they are legally obligated to do it. WE NEED MINUTEMEN TO BEGIN THIS ACTION. WILL YOU HELP? Consider this fact. Most of The Mountain Man's sources show how the blood line of family bankers who own the FED funded both sides of all major wars since American began. They created fake colonial money to destroy the Americans during the Revolutionary War, and tried to finance both sides in the American Civil War. Abraham Lincoln refused, and the South accepted. Many publications show that these bankers financed World War I, World War II, and the Russian Revolutionary War, which helped Napoleon, Lenin, and Hitler come to power.

They financed both sides from money created from nothing and profited greatly in return. These same bankers created a number of American depressions to change the U.S. legislation and seize our wealth, nurturing the "Grapes of Wrath". This is why our forefathers wrote in the Constitution that only Congress can issue money — not private banks. More wars create more debt which means more profit to the bankers. These bankers planned three world wars so people would welcome United Nations intervention to govern the world in peace, not war.

The banks have publicly announced they will force us to a cashless society whether we like it or not. Furthermore, they plan to create a One World Government through the United Nations headed by the FED, Trilaterals, and the Council on Foreign Relations. By the definition of "treason", they have committed treason! This means you lose your rights under the Constitution of the United States and the Bill of Rights. Does this sound far fetched? Twenty-four U.S. Senators (two of them presidential candidates, Harkin & Tsongas) and 80 Representatives have signed a "Declaration of Interdependence."

This Declaration, designed to make a One World Government, is treason to the oath of office they took upon entering office; and the media remained silent. The FED announced publicly that their first objective was to get "nationalism" out of the

American people's heads because patriotism to a country would not be of value in the future. The media makes us think the U.N. has all the answers and encourages to "think globally". Congress passed a law stopping certain individuals from being tried for this treason. Why pass this law if no treason was committed? State Department document 7277 calls for the disarming of America, thus turning our sovereignty over to a One-World Government.

Again, the media is pushing to eliminate guns. Our forefathers believed that the right to bear arms would prevent a takeover of our government, or a takeover of us *by* our government. History shows that before any government took over, in the past, they disarmed the citizens. Hitler did it, and before our Revolutionary War, King George told us to disarm — good thing we didn't!

Under the Federal Reserve Bank Act, the bankers control our economy. The FED controls interest rates and the amount of money in the economy. These factors determine either economic prosperity or the lack thereof. Bankers are now pushing for a One World Government and a cashless society. Why cashless? No cash means no money for drugs, no theft, and the ability to collect taxes on the underground economy. Anyone who wouldn't support a cashless society must be a drug dealer, thief, or tax evader, right? Wrong! What a cashless society really means is the banks can now control you. Today you fear the IRS. In a cashless society, if you disagree with the bankers' political goals, you'll find your money gone via "computer error".

If you could accurately predict future interest rates, inflation and deflation, you would know when to buy or sell stocks and make a bundle of money. The FED has secret meetings (according to the Congressional Record) to determine future interest rates and the amount of money to be printed. The Securities Exchange Commission (SEC) by law, stops insiders from profiting by privileged information. Congressional records prove that FED bankers routinely hold secret meetings to profit by manipulating the stock market via interest rates and the amount of money they create. FED bankers also profit greatly from economic disasters like the Depression. The bankers create inflation, sell their stocks before the market crashes, then buy up those very stocks at lower prices. Bankers admitted this to Congress. This violates the law, yet Congress does not act, because these bankers are large political contributors. Thomas Jefferson predicted this scenario if we ever allowed a private bank, like the FED, to create our currency.

FED Chairman Burns states *"A financial killing can be made simply by knowing the next few months newspapers ahead of time."* Congressman Patman said *"The FED officials own more than 100 million dollars (of stocks) while making decisions influencing these stock prices..."*

Congress consistently defeats balanced budget amendments. In the past 30 years, Congress has raised our taxes 56 times and balanced the budget only once. We need the sound banking system our forefathers wanted us to have. History proves that banking systems like the FED don't work. Major world powers have been destroyed over similar banking systems. If we don't change this system NOW, the only thing our taxes will eventually pay is the interest on the national debt.

Section 7 of the Federal Reserve Act, passed December 23, 1913, states that much of the profit of the FED should flow into the U.S. Treasury. In 1959, new legislation allowed the FED to transfer bonds to commercial banks at no cost to the bank. Now the FED receives less interest income and less profit for the U.S. Treasury because the money is diverted to other banks through an accounting entry. Congress and the IRS do not have access to the financial records of the FED.

Every year Congress introduces legislation to audit the FED and every year it is defeated. The FED banking system could easily be netting $100s of billions in profit each year. Through "creative accounting" profit can easily be reclassified as expense. Within the first few years, the shareholders of the FED received their initial investment back with no risk. All the income is tax-free, except for property tax, according to the Federal Reserve Act. When are the profits of the FED going to start flowing into the Treasury so that average Americans are no longer burdened with excessive, unnecessary taxes? Clearly, Congress cannot or will not control the FED.

IT IS TIME TO ABOLISH THE FED!

Chapter 12
Abolish The Federal Reserve

RESOLUTION of the MOUNTAIN MAN condemning the economic control over the Citizens of Mitchell County, State of North Carolina, by the Federal Reserve Board, the policy-making agency of the Federal Reserve System, a consortium of private bankers, and demands that the North Carolina State legislature shall protect the money and property of Mitchell County citizens as it is required to do under provisions of the State Constitution and the Constitution of the United States, by instructing members of the North Carolina Congressional Delegation to jointly sponsor legislation to repeal the Federal Reserve Act, as they are authorized to do under Article 30 (now 31) of the original Federal Reserve Act.

THE MOUNTAIN MAN FINDS that Article 1, Section 8, of the Constitution of the United States provides that only the Congress of the United States shall have the power "to borrow money on the credit of the United States."

THE MOUNTAIN MAN FINDS that Article 1, Section 8, of the Constitution of the United States provides that only the Congress of the United States is permitted to "coin money, regulate the value thereof, and of foreign coin."

THE MOUNTAIN MAN FINDS that the Federal Reserve Act (Act of December 1913; 38 Sat. 251; 12 United States Code section 221, et. seq.) purported to transfer the power to borrow money on the credit of the United States, and the power to coin money and regulate the value thereof to a consortium of private bankers, i.e.; the Federal Reserve System, in violation of the prohibitions of Article 1, Section 8, of the Constitution of the United States.

THE MOUNTAIN MAN FINDS that Article 1, Section 1, of the Constitution of the United States provides that "all legislative powers herein granted shall be vested in the Congress of the United States, which shall consist of a Senate and House of Representatives."

THE MOUNTAIN MAN FINDS that Article 1, Section 8, of the Constitution of the United States is without authority to delegate any powers which it has received from the people under the constitutional contract.

THE MOUNTAIN MAN FINDS that the Federal Reserve Act of 23 December 1913 was imposed upon the Citizens of Mitchell Country, State of North Carolina, in violation of Article 1, Section 1, of the Constitution of the United States.

THE MOUNTAIN MAN FINDS that the Federal Reserve System which is not subject to any official periodic review or oversight by Congress, has unconstitutionally controlled the economy of the United States and financial fortunes of Mitchell County citizens, State of North Carolina, through the alleged powers of the Federal Reserve Act unconstitutionally granted by the Congress of the United States.

THE MOUNTAIN MAN FINDS that the citizens of Mitchell County, State of North Carolina, face economic crisis under hardship brought about by the unconstitutional, arbitrary, and capricious control and management of the nation's money supply by the Federal Reserve Board, the policy making agency of the Federal Reserve System, a consortium of private bankers.

THE MOUNTAIN MAN CONDEMNS economic control over the citizens of Mitchell Country by the Federal Reserve Board, and demands that the North Carolina State Legislature shall instruct the members of the North Carolina Congressional Delegation to jointly sponsor legislation to repeal the Federal Reserve Act of 23 December 1913, as they are authorized to do under Article 30 (now 31) of the original act.

THE MOUNTAIN MAN URGES the North Carolina legislature to take whatever action may be necessary to protect the money and property of Mitchell County citizens, State of North Carolina, as it is required to do under provisions of the North Carolina State Constitution and the Constitution of the United States.

THE MOUNTAIN MAN PETITIONS that a copy of this Resolution, be forwarded to the State Legislative Delegation, Majority Leader of Senate and House, Governor, Lieutenant Governor, Secretary of State, Attorney General, and the President, State Association of County Commissioners, State of North Carolina, requesting enabling legislation.

THE FOREGOING RESOLUTION was introduced by a motion of **THE MOUNTAIN MAN**, seconded, and a vote taken that carried the motion.

This the 1st day of January, 200?

THE MOUNTAIN MAN
Committee Chairman

RESOLUTION EPILOGUE

The people, from whom flow all political authority, are responsible for instructing their elected officials to confine the functions of government to limitations defined in articles of the Constitution of the United States.

State lawmakers are required to take whatever action is necessary to enforce the provisions of the Constitution of the United States.

Chapter 13
Emergancy War Powers Act Of 1933

"The capitalist does not know the real definition of war. He thinks of war as an attack with force and machines. He does not know that a more effective, if somewhat longer war can be fought with bread, or with drugs, and the wisdom of our art." — Communist Levrenti Pavlovich Beria.

The following information pertains to the synthesis on brainwashing found in the Russian textbook on PSYCHOPOLITICS by Lavrenti Pavlovich Berea, head of the Soviet Secret Police and right hand man to Joseph Stalin. Psychopolitics is the art and science of capturing the mind of a nation by brainwashing — by controlling the thoughts and loyalties of individuals, officers, bureaus and masses by subjecting whole nations of people to the Antichrist of hypnotic control — by capturing and controlling their minds.

"By psychopolitics our chief goal is to produce chaos in the culture of the enemy, our first and most important step. Our fruits are grown in chaos, distrust, turmoil, and distress." — Beria.

The mind is controlled either with truth or with error. And when the mind is controlled by another's will one becomes the involuntary accomplice to and agent of his schemes. Outward utterances of falsehood are openly met with rebuttal, but the evil method of injuring others by a silent and subtle impregnation of lies in the mind is "Satan let loose" — the sin that "standeth in the holy place." More subtle than all the beasts of the field, it coils itself about the sleeper, fastening its fangs in innocence while killing in the dark. Every loyal American should be aware of the fact that: **it is not always by armies and guns that a nation is conquered.**

"One must in an entire country create and continue a semi-privation in the masses in order to command and utterly control the nation." — Beria.

In 1910 the plans for the economic takeover of America were set in place. On November 22, a few notable financiers secretly met at the lavish J. P. Morgan estate on Jekyll's island off the coast of Georgia [ostensibly for duck hunting] to prepare a bill for Congress which was later submitted as the Aldrich Plan. When resistance to this plan arose in the House of Representatives where an official investigation had revealed some of the ruthless operations of powerful financial interests on Wall Street resulting in the financial crash of 1908, strategy was then switched to an alternate plan that was in essence the Aldrich Plan but with a different name: the Federal Reserve Act.

"Every rich man, every statesman, every person well informed and capable in government must have brought to his side as a trusted confidant a psychopolitical operator. Communism can best succeed if at the side of every rich or influential man there would be placed a psychopolitical operator who could then by his advice and guided opinions direct the optimum policies of the country. Planted beside a country's powerful persons, the psychopolitical operator can guide other policies to the betterment of our designs." — Beria.

When Woodrow Wilson took over the White House in 1913, he brought with him his trusted Wall Street advisor, Colonel Edward Mandell House, who became the major policy maker and manager of the entire Wilson administration. And on December 22, 1913, three days before Christmas, Congress authorized the establishment of the new Federal Reserve System, also referred to as the Currency Bill. By that action, the financial system of the United States was surrendered to the Federal Reserve Board — the rulers of a purely profiteering group of bankers that were and are mainly interested in obtaining profits from the use of "other people's money".

"In a nation under conquest, our slow and stealthy approach need take advantage only of the cycles of booms and busts in order to assert more control over individual wills. The masses can thus be brought to accept such a thing as an income tax, a Marxist principle smoothly slid into the capitalistic framework of the United States in 1910; this even though the basic law of the United States [the U.S. Constitution] forbade it, and even though Communism at that time had been active only a few years in America." — Beria.

Without realizing it, Congress created the powerful engine of private central banking which was surreptitiously given the power to control boom-and-bust cycles and the nation's money supply, smothering the nation with indebtedness and the promotions of war on a world-wide scale — the power to confiscate the peoples' gold, diminish their savings, erode away the value of insurance policies and fixed incomes, and destroy the stability of the dollar through printing press inflation and the unconstitutional federal income tax, and engulf the nation in a miasma of foreign entanglements that would threaten the very existence of the United States as a free and independent people.

"Without rigorous and forthright control there can be no accomplished goals for the state. Without force and threat there can be no striving. Without pain there can be no desire to escape pain. All goals proceed from duress." — Beria.

At the height of the duress and pain of the Great Depression of the early 1930's, the Federal Reserve Board of New York drafted presidential Executive Order 39 before Herbert Hoover left office in 1933. And when the Federal Reserve Board fostered this Executive Order on Herbert Hoover, on the final day of his Presidency, Hoover refused to sign it because he saw no Constitutional authority for such an order. But three days later, on his second day in office, Franklin Delano Roosevelt did signed it and declared a "national state of emergency" calling all the Governors to Washington D.C. where — with the Governors' approval but without a copy of it and without reading it — Congress passed the Emergency Banking Relief Act of 1933, on March 9. This Act delegated all the Emergency Relief Act powers to the President, and Congress retroactively confirmed his earlier declaration of war that he was never Constitutionally authorized to make.

In so doing, the very people who had sworn to protect the Constitutional liberties of the people of the United States, went along with the "usurper" under cover of this so-called "emergency" which was supposed to be temporary. Not only did the Legislators of Congress go along with this fateful Act, but the Governors of the states as well. All the Governors went back home to declare, within each and every state, emergency "remedies of uniform application" (Act of March 9, 1933, preamble). These became the Uniform Rules of National Application: the Declarations of State Emergencies of 1933.

The basis for this "emergency" scheme was the Trading With the Enemies Act of 1917 that Congress passed during the First World War. This act recognized the existence of enemies of the United States within the continental United States. This act delegated to the President (at that time) total authoritarian control (dictatorial power) over all the finances of the then internal "enemies" of the United States. By this act the President was given the power to control all the enemy alien's monetary transactions and he had to license ("permit an otherwise illegal act") everything they did.

This is a critically important point because once a country declares another country's citizens as enemies, then under the Law of Nations everything that an enemy alien does within the belligerent country becomes illegal unless the enemy alien obtains a license from the federal government.

This act did not apply to the American people; they were exempt from its power. This act applied to German citizens and German citizens and Corporations of Germany's allies only during the First World War because the Trading With the Enemy Act terminated at the end of the war in 1918. It didn't apply to American citizens in any way until this law and was unlawfully revived to support the socialization of America through Roosevelt's New Deal starting in 1933.

Since 1933 we've lived under the dictates of a government that controls everything we do — our money, our finances, and our economic and social lives as well. By these "emergency powers" the federal government extended its jurisdiction inland and usurped the states' domestic jurisdictions. The federal government now decrees what our children should or should not eat; that all newly delivered mothers must stay in the hospital two days; and that we should "protect" the spotted owl and the Delhi Sands fly (etc.), and the rivers and parks in our own back yard!

The jokes on us! America's been had!

For the past 60 and more years (more than a whole generation) America has lived in a so-called state of war. A "state of emergency" that was declared in 1933 while we were still under the protections of the Constitution of the United States. On March 9, 1933, Congress passed the Emergency Relief Act and turned America over to our enemy! Article 1, Section 8 of the Constitution says that only Congress shall have the power to declare war. There was no war but that was the authority Roosevelt claimed and usurped through presidential Executive Order 39.

"In a capitalist state you are aided on all sides by the corruptions of the philosophy of man and the times. Everything will aid you in your campaign to seize control, and you will discover that you can now effect your own legislation at will, by constant campaigns about the terrors of society, and make your capitalist himself, by his own appropriations, finance a large portion of our quiet communist conquest of the nation." — Beria.

Franklin Delano Roosevelt was inaugurated as President of the United States on March 4, 1933. To prepare the way for his "takeover" of the nation; he called all the state Governors to an emergency conclave in Washington D.C., who at his urging unanimously passed two resolutions that gave away the United States to a foreign-instigated takeover of socialistic design. The Crown of England once again prevailed through these resolutions, taking their former Colony back unto themselves — and the forceful effect of our Declaration of Independence was no more; for richer or for poorer unto death.

First, the Governor's, by resolution, pledged the whole hearted support of all states to Roosevelt's full use of broad unconstitutional powers to deal with the Federal Reserve instigated "emergency".

Secondly, the Governors passed another resolution for Congress to pass a bill delegating the so-called "war powers" to the President, which became his "war-power" emergency declaration: presidential Executive Order 39. We know it as the Bank Holiday Proclamation of 1933 through which he seized control of all of the nation's banks and control of the nation itself on the basis of totally unconstitutional authority.

The Emergency Relief Act (ERA) was followed by The Emergency Agricultural Adjustment Act (EAAA); the National Industrial Recovery Act (NIRA); The Emergency Relief and Employment Act (EREA), and all the other Public Welfare Acts of 1933, whereby the federal government authorized and gave to the states "grants-in-aid" [booty?] to pay for all these socializing programs, and in so agreeing to these socialistic programs, the states surrendered their sovereignty to the federal Government and agreed to be, thereafter, federal Government pawns!

"You can change loyalties by psychopolitics. Given a short time with a psychopolitician, you can alter forever the loyalty of a statesman or leader in his own country, or you can destroy his mind." — Beria.

The states which had heretofore ruled the federal Government, became agents of the federal Government for the duration of a conjured "emergency" that has existed since 1933. Upon declaration of "war" the federal Government became our Master, the states became agents of the federal Government, and every county in every state became agents of the State! All this the result of a totally controlled and centrally planned agenda, economical and social as well. It was a reimplementation of Hoover's World War I Government; not strictly fascism but almost. It was a coup d'etat seizure of power by a revolutionary government headed by F.D.R. It overthrew the Constitution and introduced a new monetary system and cartelized all agriculture, labor, and business, under the federal umbrella of one big socialist Commune! Then all the state Governors went back home and did the same thing on the state level. To make programs like the National Industrial Recovery Act (NIRA) lawful within the states, every state had to suspend its anti-monopoly and anti-trust laws as part of their NIRA acts, and every state did just that!

Within four years (by 1937) Roosevelt's New Deal was failing; it couldn't deliver the promised Recovery. The Supreme Court overturned most of it except the money provision, the Congress passed similar but slightly different legislation, and F.D.R. reappointed Supreme Court Justices and stacked the Supreme Court in his favor. So the "emergency" Government continued even though it wasn't working very well, or not at all. Then World War II gave Roosevelt the excuse to continue and instigate even greater deficit spending to prepare for and help in the war. This provided the means to escape the Great Depression. And once World War II started, anyone who disagreed with F.D.R.'s fascist state was prima facie [at face value] a "traitor" to America. This silenced those who had disagreed with Roosevelt's administration before the *real* war began. And America has been operating in a state of siege — the equivalent of a state of war — ever since.

The irony of this, is that *"One of the most significant facts about the New Deal was its orthodoxy on money. For the whole twelve years that he was in the White House, Roosevelt had statutory power to issue money in the form of greenbacks, by the government without recourse to the banks [as Abraham Lincoln had done during the Civil War]. This authority was never used....the emergency of the war in 1942 made it possible to justify a limitless increase in the national debt by limitless borrowing from private persons <u>and the banks</u>. But the whole episode showed a failure to grasp the nature of money and the function of the monetary system, of which considerable traces remained in the postwar period."* — Carroll Quigley, *Tragedy and Hope,* page 534.

Quigley is in fact saying that the insiders actually do *"grasp the nature of money and the function of the monetary system"*. The main problem of the Great Depression and of the subsequent New Deal, was simply the *intentional* lack of available cash to conduct the business and lives of the nation's people. The financiers brought economic pressure to bear on the nation by their "lack of confidence" [refusal!] to release their large unused coffers into economic investment, and the "debt money" system was intentionally retained.

Three months before Roosevelt's declaration of emergency war, Hitler had declared a "state of emergency" in Germany and assumed the same powers, under Article 48 of the Constitution of the Weimar Republic. This same tactic — depression followed by panic — was used to install Corporativist [Socialist] governments all over the Western World within the G-7 Countries: Canada, France, Germany, Great Britain, Italy, Japan, and the United States.

In the G-7 Nations, we don't sign treaties any more — we sign "executive agreements". On June 12, 1934, Congress passed the International Trade Agreements Act "to promote foreign trade" and "to help bring us out of the Great Depression". This authorized the President, on his own prerogative and without Congressional interference, to make agreements with foreign nations. These are now called "executive agreements"; they are not treaties. NAFTA and GATT are not treaties but were passed under "fast track" where the President makes all the arrangements.

In 1976, Congress restricted some of the President's powers and took oversight control. That's why Congress and the Senate passed NAFTA and GATT by simple majority votes.

Under the Constitution (Article 11, Section 2) the President "shall have power to make treaties by and with the advice and consent of the Senate." But *these* were not treaties, these were "executive agreements" under the War Powers Act.

Congress is allowing this abnormal and extaconstitutional "state of emergency" because there has been little or no challenge to this condition. Mainly because most people aren't aware that this condition exists. As a result, no President or Congressman, and consequently no State has stood up in opposition. The states can stand up and interpose between the federal government and the people if they are so inclined to do.

F.D.R. knew he had to get the Governors' approval before he declared the Emergency before he could carry out his takeover of America. Otherwise all his acts and powers would have been unlawful within the states. The states abdicated their rights and the rights of the individuals within the states, in 1933.

The states passed those acts of Congress and they can repeal them the same way they passed them, so that they become unlawful within the states during times of peace, simply by declaring, "We hereby find that the emergency is terminated."

But if a state passes a resolution terminating the "emergency", they would suddenly bring a stop to welfare and all other federal social programs; this would turn American life upside down. Once a state or the states as a whole terminate their so-called emergencies, we'll see a whole new concept of freedom take hold — but possibly rioting in the streets if done too quickly. So we can't terminate immediately without a well thought out plan to prepare the way for a smooth transition from more than sixty years of "emergency" government, back to the Constitutional government intended by the Founders of our Country. And there are people who are talking about this today. In the federal government, in state governments, and even within and without the Federal Reserve.

Why would people in the Federal Reserve want to give up that emergency power? Because in the long run it simply cannot work; the whole country's heading for collapse.

This emergency money, and emergency system cannot work forever. We've built houses and roads, and bridges and damns, and weapons of war and institutions for peace, etc. — but nothing is paid for! It has all been done with debt. And this will make a critical difference to future generations and possibly to us.

All this debt is a mortgage on America bearing ever increasing interest. Eventually this interest will reach a point where we can't generate enough new money to pay that interest, then the burden of debt will become so great that the people will simply cease to perform and the whole system will collapse inward upon itself. We're seeing evidences of that happening today! Like what's happened all ready in Russia, even now; complete economic collapse because there's no incentive to perform otherwise.

Most people who work for governments or universities, or the Federal Reserve, just work for wages like everybody else. If this country's economy collapses it will severely hurt political unity and the political base that supports the current government. We can't continue to increase the debt indefinitely, sinking future generations deeper and deeper in debt; this "game of chance" cannot go on forever.

The Emergency Powers issue sounds complicated at first, but once you understand what's happening, it becomes clear how the federal government — external to the states and without any original domestic jurisdiction within the states — has expanded its jurisdiction into the states so that we now have federal agents involved in everything we do — like in "Waco" and "Ruby Ridge".

Under the Emergency Powers statutes federal police power — (or federal military power, or standing army power) — is being extended into the states. We have a war-time government; not a peace-time one, and "we the people" are the enemy at large. We have found the enemy; and it is us! The only issue is our so-called "national survival"; all Constitutional restraints go by the board until the issue of national survival is resolved. But how?

Our forefathers based the Declaration of Independence on the Magna Carta of 1215 which was our Constitution prior to the Revolutionary War with our own government: England. Chapter 61 says that whenever the government jumps the bonds of the Constitution, the people should assemble and petition the government for redress of grievances; laying out the specific causes of duress to be addressed. In 1774 our forefathers assembled in the First Continental Congress and drafted the first petition of redress: The Declaration of Rights.

We still retain all the rights of the Magna Carta and Chapter 61 was specifically carried forward into our American Constitution as the First Amendment. "Congress shall make no laws abridging the right of the people peaceably to assemble and petition the government for a redress of grievances."

We can call for an assembly of the people. And in that assembly we can present all the evidence that we have, and from that, draft a petition of redress and serve it on all government officials: our Country Commissioners, our Legislators, the Governor, the Attorney General, Court Justices and Appellate Court Justices, and then call for a permanent "standing committee" by resolution, to study and report how to terminate the "emergency" in North Carolina.

In an Amendment Resolution, the State of North Carolina can declare that the State had only given the federal Government powers that are specifically granted in the Constitution of the United States, and that all other powers are reserved to the states and the people respectively.

The law presumes that the federal Government acted out of necessity without malice or criminal intent. How do we determine intent? We assemble and petition for redress.

The law demands that we offer notice and grace. The petition is the notice that the law requires, then we provide the grace — time and opportunity to cure the actions of which we complain. We don't want conflict; we want reconciliation. We want the problems fixed so we can establish freedom and prosperity according to the Constitution of these United States.

The Constitution provides that only Congress has the power to declare war; whether good or bad is beside the point. As long as the war is on, the Courts must uphold Congress' Emergency Statues. If the people think it is a bad war they can have Congress terminate the war. When we read the Constitution and our history, everything becomes clear.

APPENDIX

Executive Orders Farce

An Executive Order is an order issued by a government executive on the basis of authority specifically granted to the executive branch of the government. An executive order from the president does not have the force of law until it is printed in the Federal Register.

President Clinton is ruling America by Executive Order. Since he was sworn into office, in 1992, he has issued more than 200 of these fiat directives. This is dictatorial rule by decree — no different than the absolute rule of a king. These instruments of law are wholly unconstitutional in their concept, but used and abused under the **War and Emergency Powers Act of March 9, 1933.** Ever since Frankllin Delano Roosevelt, presidents have been by-passing Congress and the Constitution leaving us with a dictatorship.

With the **War and Emergency Powers Act of 1933** FDR issued Executive Orders that literally suspended the Constitution that he was sworn to uphold and defend, and we have been controlled under quasi-military marshal law ever since — for the past some 66 years. America is but a heartbeat away from being a totalitarian dictatorship. **Presidential Decision Directive 25** (**PDD-25**), regarding our American military serving under the United Nation's flag and command, is an impeachable offense.

America has been under a state of emergency since March 9, 1933. This has been upheld and continued by 5 Democratic and 5 Republican presidents since that time, Clinton being the most recent and most aggressive. This unlawful justification has deceptively allowed presidents to exercise dictatorial powers not allowed them under the Constitution of these United States.

The Powers And Duties Of Congress

In the June 1997 issue of *The John Birch Society Bulletin*, constitutional analyst Don Fotheringham created an invaluable reference by listing all of the enumerated powers and duties of Congress. That list, which should be at the fingertips of every congressman, follows.

1. Levy taxes.

2. Borrow money on the credit of the United States.

3. Spend.

4. Pay the federal debts.

5. Conduct tribunals inferior to the Supreme Court.

6. Declare war.

7. Raise armies, a navy, and provide for the common defense.

8. Introduce constitutional amendments and choose the mode of ratification.

9. Call a convention on the application of two-thirds of the states.

10. Regulate interstate and foreign commerce.

11. Coin money.

12. Regulate (standardize) the value of currency.

13. Regulate patents and copyrights.

14. Establish federal courts lower than the Supreme Court.

15. Limit the appellate jurisdiction of the federal courts, including the Supreme Court.

16. Standardize weights and measures.

17. Establish uniform times for elections.

18. Control the postal system.

19. Establish laws governing citizenship.

20. Make its own rules and discipline its own members.

21. Provide for the punishment of counterfeiting, piracy, treason, and other federal crimes.

22. Exercise exclusive jurisdiction over the District of Columbia.

23. Establish bankruptcy laws.

24. Override presidential vetoes.

25. Oversee all federal property and possessions.

26. Fill a vacancy in the Presidency in cases of death or inability.

27. Receive electoral votes for the Presidency.

28. Keep and publish a journal of its proceedings.

29. Conduct a census every ten years

30. Approve treaties, Cabinet-level appointments, and appointments to the Supreme Court (Senate only).

31. Impeach (House only) and try (Senate only) federal officers.

32. Initiate all bills for raising revenue (House only).

These are the powers of Congress; there are no non-enumerated powers. Leaving nothing to inference, the Constitution even specifies that Congress may pass the laws "necessary and proper" for executing its specified powers. Congressmen have simply to study and apply the Constitution in order to restore sound government. That most fail to do so is not the fault of the Founders, but of the people who elect the congressmen and send them to Washington.

Treason In Congress
A special chapter by Claire Wolfe

"Whatever we do, we must remember that we are all already, outlaws." — *Claire Wolfe*

Let me run by you a brief list of items that are "the law" in America today. As you read, consider what all these have in common.
 1. A national database of employed people. For the time being there will be zero (count 'em, zero) privacy safeguards on this data.
 2. 100 pages of new "health care crimes," for which the penalty is (among other things) seizure of assets from both doctors and patients.
 3. Confiscation of assets from any American who establishes foreign citizenship.
 4. The largest gun confiscation in U.S. history—which is also an unconstitutional ex post facto law and the first law ever to remove people's constitutional rights for committing a misdemeanor.
 5. A law banning guns in ill-defined school zones; random roadblocks may be used for enforcement; gun-bearing residents could become federal criminals just by stepping outside their doors or getting into vehicles.
 6. Increased funding for the Bureau of Alcohol, tobacco and Firearms, an agency infamous for its brutality, dishonesty and ineptitude.
 7. A law enabling the executive branch to declare various groups "terrorist"—without stating any reason and without the possibility of appeal. Once a group has been so declared, its mailing and membership lists must be turned over to the government.

8. A law authorizing secret trials with secret evidence for certain classes of people.

9. A law requiring that all states begin issuing drivers' licenses carrying Social Security numbers and "security features" (such as magnetically coded fingerprints and personal records) by October 1, 2000. By October 1, 2006, "Neither the Social Security Administration nor the Passport Office nor any other federal agency nor any state nor local government agency may accept for any evidentiary purpose a state driver's license or identification document in a form other than [one issued with a verified Social Security number and 'security features']."

10. And my personal favorite—a national database, now being constructed, that will contain every exchange and observation that takes place in your doctor's office. This includes records of your prescriptions, your hemorrhoids and your mental illness. It also includes—by law—any statements you make ("Doc, I'm worried my kid may be on drugs," "Doc, I've been so stressed out lately I feel about ready to go postal.") and any observations your doctor makes about your mental or physical condition, whether accurate or not, whether made with your knowledge or not. For the time being, there will be zero (count >em, zero) privacy safeguards on this data. But don't worry, your government will protect you with some undefined "privacy standards" — in a few years.

All of the above items are the law of the land. Federal law. What else do they have in common?

Well, when I ask this question to audiences, I usually get the answer, "They're all unconstitutional."

True.

My favorite answer came from an eloquent college student who blurted, "They all SUUUCK!"

Also true.

But the saddest and most telling answer is: They were all the product of the 104th Congress. Every one of the horrors above was imposed upon you by the Congress of the Republican Revolution — the Congress that pledged to "get government off your back."

BURYING TIME BOMBS

All of the above became law by being buried in larger bills. In many cases, they are hidden sneak attacks upon individual liberties that were neither debated on the floor of Congress nor reported in the media.

For instance, three of the most horrific items (the health care database, asset confiscation for foreign residency and the 100 pages of health care crimes) were hidden in the Kennedy-Kassebaum Health Insurance Portability and Accountability Act of 1996 (H.R. 3103). You didn't hear about them at the time because the media was too busy celebrating this "moderate, compromise" bill that "simply" ensured that no American would ever lose insurance coverage due to a job change or a preexisting condition.

Your legislator may not have heard about them either. Because he or she didn't care enough to do so.

The fact is, most legislators don't even read the laws they inflict upon the public. They read the title of the bill (which may be something like "The Save the Sweet Widdle Babies from Gun Violence by Drooling Drug Fiends Act of 1984"). They read summaries, which are often prepared by the very agencies or groups pushing the bill. And they vote according to various deals or pressures. The Constitution, your legislator's oath to it, and your inalienable rights (which precede the Constitution) never entered into anyone's consideration.

It also sometimes happens that the most horrible provisions are sneaked into bills during conference committee negotiations, after both House and Senate have voted on their separate versions of the bills. The conference committee process is supposed simply to reconcile differences between two versions of a bill. But power brokers use it for purposes of their own, adding what they wish. Then members of the House and Senate vote on the final, unified version of the bill, often in a great rush, and often without even having the amended text available for review.

I have even heard (though I cannot verify) that stealth provisions are written into some bills after all the voting has taken place. Someone with a hidden agenda simply edits them in to suit his or her own purposes. So these time bombs become "law" without ever having been voted on by anybody. And who's to know? If congresspeople don't even read legislation before they vote on it, why would they bother reading it afterward? Are power brokers capable of such chicanery? Do we even need to ask? Is the computer system in which bills are stored vulnerable to tampering by people within or outside of Congress? We certainly should ask.

Whether your legislators were ignorant of the infamy they were perpetrating, or whether they knew, one thing is absolutely certain: the Constitution, your legislator's oath to it, and your inalienable rights (which precede the Constitution) never entered into anyone's consideration.

Ironically, you may recall that one of the early pledges of Newt Gingrich and Company was to stop these stealth attacks. Very early in the 104th Congress, the Republican leadership declared that, henceforth, all bills would deal only with the subject matter named in the title of the bill.

When, at the beginning of the first session of the 104th, pro-gun Republicans attempted to attach a repeal of the "assault weapons" ban to another bill, House leaders dismissed their amendment as not being "germane."

After that self-righteous and successful attempt to prevent pro-freedom stealth legislation, Congresspeople turned right around and got back to the dirty old business of practicing all the anti-freedom stealth they were capable of.

STEALTH ATTACKS IN BROAD DAYLIGHT

Three other items on my list (ATF funding, gun confiscation

and school zone roadblocks) were also buried in a big bill—H.R. 3610, the budget appropriation passed near the end of the second session of the 104th Congress.

No legislator can claim to have been unaware of these three because they were brought to public attention by gun-rights groups and hotly debated in both Congress and the media. Yet some 90 percent of all congresspeople voted for them—including many who claim to be ardent 'protectors' of the rights guaranteed by the Second Amendment.

Why?

Well, in the case of my wrapped-in-the-flag, allegedly pro-gun Republican congressman: "Bill Clinton made me do it!"

Okay, I paraphrase. What she actually said was more like, "It was part of a budget appropriations package. The public got mad at us for shutting the government down in 1994. If we hadn't voted for this budget bill, they might have elected a Democratic legislature in 1996—and you wouldn't want THAT, would you?"

Oh heavens, no! I'd much rather be enslaved by people who spell their name with an R. than people who spell their name with a D. Makes all the difference in the world!

HOW SNEAK ATTACKS ARE JUSTIFIED

The Republicans are fond of claiming that Bill Clinton "forced" them to pass certain legislation by threatening to veto anything they sent to the White House that didn't meet his specs.

In other cases (as with the Kennedy-Kassebaum bill), they proudly proclaim their misdeeds in the name of bipartisanship — while carefully forgetting to mention the true nature of what they're doing.

In still others, they trumpet their triumph over the evil Democrats and claim the mantle of limited government while sticking it to us and to the Constitution. The national database of "workers" was in the welfare reform bill they "forced" Clinton to accept. The requirement for S.S. numbers and ominous "security" devices on drivers licenses originated in their very own Immigration Control and Financial Responsibility Act of 1996, H.R. 2202.

Another common trick, called to my attention by Redmon Barbry, publisher of the electronic magazine *Fratricide*, is to hide duplicate or near-duplicate provisions in several bills. Then, when the Supreme Court declares Section A of Law Z to be unconstitutional, its kissing cousin, Section B of Law Y, remains to rule us.

Sometimes this particular form of trickery is done even more brazenly; when the Supreme Court, in its Lopez decision, declared federal-level school zone gun bans unconstitutional because Congress demonstrated no jurisdiction, Congress brassily changed a few words. They claimed that school zones fell under the heading of "interstate commerce." Then they sneaked the provision into H.R. 3610, where it became "law" once again.

When angry voters upbraid congresspeople about some Big Brotherish horror they've inflicted upon the country by stealth, congresspeople claim lack of knowledge, lack of time, party pressure, public pressure, or they justify themselves by claiming that the rest of the bill was "good."

The simple fact is that, regardless of what reasons legislators may claim, the U.S. Congress has passed more Big Brother legislation in the last two years — more laws to enable tracking, spying and controlling — than any Democratic congress ever passed. And they have done it, in large part, in secret.

Redmon Barbry put it best: "We the people have the right to expect our elected representatives to read, comprehend and master the bills they vote on. If this means Congress passes only 50 bills per session instead of 5,000, so be it. As far as I am concerned, whoever subverts this process is committing treason."

By whatever means the deed is done, there is no acceptable excuse for voting against the Constitution, voting for tyranny. And I would add to Redmon's comments: those who *do* read the bills, then knowingly vote to ravage our liberties, are *doubly* guilty. But when do the treason trials begin?

BILLS AS WINDOW DRESSING FOR AN UGLY AGENDA

The truth is that these tiny, buried provisions are often the real intent of the law, and that the hundred, perhaps thousands, of pages that surround them are sometimes nothing more than elaborate window dressing. These tiny time bombs are placed there at the behest of federal police agencies or other power groups whose agenda is not clearly visible to us. And their impact is felt long after the outward intent of the bill has been forgotten.

Civil forfeiture — now one of the plagues of the nation — was first introduced in the 1970s as one of those buried, almost unnoticed provisions of a larger law.

One wonders why on earth a "health care bill" carried a provision to confiscate the assets of people who become frightened or discouraged enough to leave the country. (In fact, the entire bill was an amendment to the Internal Revenue Code. Go figure.)

But when do the treason trials begin?

I think we all realize by now that that database of employed people will still be around enabling government to track our locations (and heaven knows what else about us, as the database is enhanced and expanded) long after the touted benefits of "welfare reform" have failed to materialize.

And most grimly of all, our drivers' licenses will be our de facto national ID card long after immigrants have ceased to want to come to this Land of Once Free.

CONTROL REIGNS

It matters not one whit whether the people controlling you call themselves R's or D's, liberals or conservatives, socialists or even (I hate to admit) libertarians. It doesn't matter whether they vote for these horrors because they're not paying attention or because they actually like such things.

What matters is that the pace of totalitarianism is increasing. And it is coming closer to our daily lives all the time. Once your state passes the enabling legislation (under threat of losing "federal welfare dollars"), it is YOUR name and Social Security number that will be entered in that employee database the moment you go to work for a new employer. It is YOU who will be unable to cash a check, board an airplane, get a passport or be allowed any dealings with any government agency if you refuse to give your S.S. number to the drivers license bureau. It is YOU who will be endangered by driving "illegally" if you refuse to submit to Big Brother's licensing procedures.

It is YOU whose psoriasis, manic depression or prostate troubles will soon be the reading matter of any bureaucrat with a computer. It is YOU who could be declared a member of a "foreign terrorist" organization just because you bought a book or concert tickets from some group the government doesn't like. It is YOU who could lose your home, bank account and reputation because you made a mistake on a health insurance form. Finally, when you become truly desperate for freedom, it is YOU whose assets will be seized if you try to flee this increasingly insane country.

The only way we're going to get off this road to Hell is if we jump off. If we personally, as individuals, refuse to cooperate with evil.

As Ayn Rand said in *Atlas Shrugged,* "There's no way to rule innocent men. The only power government has is the power to crack down on criminals. Well, when there aren't enough criminals, one makes them. One declares so many things to be a crime that it becomes impossible for men to live without breaking laws."

It's time to drop any pretense. We are no longer law-abiding citizens. We have lost our law-abiding status. There are simply too many laws to abide. And because of increasingly draconian penalties and electronic tracking mechanisms, our "lawbreaking" places us and our families in greater jeopardy every day.

STOPPING RUNAWAY GOVERNMENT
The question is: What are we going to do about it?

Write a nice, polite letter to your congressperson? Hey, if you think that'll help, I've got a bridge you might be interested in buying. (And it isn't your "bridge to the future," either.)

Vote "better people" into office? Oh yeah, that's what we thought we were doing in 1994.

Work to fight one bad bill or another? Okay. What will you do about the 10 or 20 or 100 equally horrible bills that will be passed behind your back while you were fighting that little battle? And let's say you defeat a nightmare bill this year. What are you going to do when they sneak it back in, at the very last minute, in some "omnibus legislation" next year? And what about the horrors you don't even learn about until two or three years after they become law?

Should you try fighting these laws in the courts? Where do you find the resources? Where do you find a judge who doesn't have a vested interest in bigger, more powerful government? And again, for every one case decided in favor of freedom, what do you do about the 10, 20 or 100 in which the courts decide against the Bill of Rights?

Perhaps you'd consider trying to stop the onrush of these horrors with a constitutional amendment — maybe one that bans "omnibus" bills, requires that every law meet a constitutional test or requires all congresspeople to sign statements that they've read and understood every aspect of every bill on which they vote. Good luck! Good luck, first, on getting such an amendment passed. Then good luck getting our Constitution-scorning so-called "leaders" to obey it.

It is true that liberty requires eternal vigilance, and part of that vigilance has been, traditionally, keeping a watchful eye on laws and on lawbreaking lawmakers. But given the current pace of law spewing and unconstitutional regulation-writing, you could watch, plead and struggle "within the system" 24 hours a day for your entire life and end up infinitely less free than when you began. Why throw your life away on a futile effort?

Face it. If "working within the system" could halt tyranny, the tyrants would outlaw it. Why do you think they encourage you to vote, to write letters, to talk to them in public forums? It's to divert your energies. To keep you tame.

"The system" as it presently exists is nothing but a rat maze. You run around thinking you're getting somewhere. Your masters occasionally reward you with a little pellet that encourages you to believe you're accomplishing something. And in the meantime, you are as much their property and their pawn as if you were a slave. In the effort of fighting them on their terms and with their authorized and approved tools, you have given your life's energy to them as surely as if you were toiling in their cotton fields, under the lash of their overseer.

The only way we're going to get off this road to Hell is if we jump off. If we, personally, as individuals, refuse to cooperate with evil. How we do that is up to each of us. I can't decide for you, nor you for me. (Unlike congresspeople, who think they can decide for everybody.)

But this totalitarian runaway truck is never going to stop unless we stop it, in any way we can. Stopping it might include any number of things: tax resistance; public civil disobedience; wide-scale, silent non-cooperation; highly noisy non-cooperation; boycotts; secession efforts; monkey wrenching; computer hacking; dirty tricks against government agents; public shunning of employees of abusive government agencies; alternative, self-sufficient communities that provide their own medical care and utilities.

There are thousands of avenues to take, and this is something most of us still need to give more thought to before we can build an effective resistance. We will each choose the courses that are right for our own circumstances, personalities and beliefs.

Whatever we do, though, we must remember that we are all, already, outlaws. Not one of us can be certain of getting through a single day without violating some law or regulation we've never even heard of. We are all guilty in the eyes of today's "law." If someone in power chooses to target us, we can all, already, be prosecuted for something.

Whatever we do, though, we must remember that we are all, already, outlaws.

And I'm sure you know that your claims of "good intentions" won't protect you, as the similar claims of politicians protect them. Politicians are above the law. YOU are under it. Crushed under it.

When you look at it that way, we have little left to lose by breakings laws creatively and purposefully. Yes, some of us will suffer horrible consequences for our lawbreaking. It is very risky to actively resist unbridled power. It is especially risky to go public with resistance (unless hundreds of thousands publicly join us), and it becomes riskier the closer we get to tyranny. For that reason, among many others, I would never recommend any particular course of action to anyone—and I hope you'll think twice before taking "advice" from anybody about things that could jeopardize your life or well-being.

But if we don't resist in the best ways we know how — and if a good number of us don't resist loudly and publicly — all of us will suffer the much worse consequences of living under total oppression.

And whatever courses of action we choose, we must remember that this legislative "revolution" against We the People will not be stopped by politeness. It will not be stopped by requests. It will not be stopped by "working within a system" governed by those who regard us as nothing but cattle. It will not be stopped by pleading for justice from those who will resort to any degree of trickery or violence to rule us.

It will not be stopped unless we are willing to risk our lives, our fortunes and our sacred honors to stop it.

I think of the words of Winston Churchill: "If you will not fight for the right when you can easily win without bloodshed, if you will not fight when your victory will be sure and not so costly, you may come to the moment when you will have to fight with all the odds against you and only a precarious chance of survival. There may be a worse case. You may have to fight when there is no chance of victory, because it is better to perish than to live as slaves."

NOTES ON THE LAWS LISTED ABOVE:
1. (Employee database) Welfare Reform Bill, H.R. 3734; became public law 104-193 on 8/22/96; see section 453A. 2. (Health care crimes) Health Insurance Portability and Accountability Act of 1996, H.R. 3103; became public law 104-191 on 8/21/96. 3. (Asset confiscation for citizenship change) Same law as #2; see sections 511-513. 4, 5, and 6. (anti-gun laws) Omnibus Appropriations Act, H.R. 3610; became public law 104-208 on 9/30/96. 7 and 8. (Terrorism & secret trials) Anti-terrorism and Effective Death Penalty Act of 1996, S. 735; became public law 104-132 on 4/24/96; see all of Title III, specifically sections 302 and 219; also see all of Title IV, specifically sections 401, 501, 502 and 503. 9. (De facto national ID card) Began life in the Immigration Control and Financial Responsibility Act of 1996, sections 111, 118, 119, 127 and 133; was eventually folded into the Omnibus Appropriations Act, H.R. 3610 (which was itself formerly called the Defense Appropriations Act—but we wouldn't want to confuse anyone, here, would we?); became public law 104-208 on 9/30/96; see sections 656 and 657 among others. 10. (Health care database) Health Insurance Portability and Accountability Act of 1996, H.R. 3103; became public law 104-191 on 8/21/96; see sections 262, 263 and 264, among others. The various provisions that make up the full horror of this database are scattered throughout the bill and may take hours to track down.; this one is stealth legislation at its utmost sneakiest.

AND ONE FINAL NOTE:
Although I spent aggravating hours verifying the specifics of these bills (a task I swear I will never waste my life on again!), the original list of bills at the top of this article was NOT the result of extensive research. It was simply what came off the top of my head when I thought of Big Brotherish bills from the 104th Congress. For all I know, Congress has passed 10 times more of that sort of thing. In fact, the worst "law" in the list — #9, the de facto national ID card — just came to my attention as I was writing this essay, thanks to the enormous efforts of Jackie Juntti and Ed Lyon and others, who researched the law. Think of it: Thanks to congressional stealth tactics, we had the long-dreaded national ID card legislation for five months, without a whisper of discussion, before freedom activists began to find out about it. Makes you wonder what else might be lurking out there, doesn't it?

Copyrighted by Claire Wolfe. Permission to reprint freely granted, provided the article is reprinted in full and that any reprint is accompanied by this copyright statement.

The Panama Canal Giveaway
by Ruby Buchanan

WHAT EXCUSE are your elected leaders giving you for not taking action concerning our National Security in the illegal giveaway of our Panama Canal?

Where is our "right-to-know" media? Most Americans think the Canal went back to Panama or that the United States was renting it from Panama, as past President Jimmy Carter claimed. The physical transfer was made by Executive Order and took place while Congress was on recess in absence of any "legal" authority to give away America's property. Only Congress has this power, under Article 1, Section 8 of the Constitution. The power to make rules for the government and regulations of land and naval forces belongs only to Congress.

Howard Air Force Base in Panama was scheduled for hand over to Red Communist China on December 31st but the transfer *actually* took place on December 15th, 1999, — once again while Congress was in recess. The 5,300 acre all-weather jet Air Force Base with an 8,000 foot runway is now a possible base for drug interdiction, foreign air traffic control, rescue missions, pilot training, — and the once source of air cover for the Canal is now gone.

The Canal is a ghost town where only a few months ago there were 10,000 U.S. Troops. They are all gone and there is no Panamanian Army to replace them; while the Clinton administration is quick to dispatch American Troops "illegally" all over the world to places like Kosovo, Haiti, and Timor. Our troops now serve in 100 foreign communist countries, — illegally. *These* places are *not* vital to American military presence or national security. The *Canal* is vital to us yet the Clinton the southern tip of South America, saving as much as 2 weeks of transport time, not to mention the savings in the costly fuel and manpower it takes to make the trip. In warfare, time means the difference between life or death; victory or defeat.

What will this mean to America now that Communist China has control of the Canal that has been deserted and abandoned by our Military? Ask your Congressman and Senators what their plans are for keeping the Canal safe in the future?

This illegal action now makes the Canal vulnerable to attack groups like "narco-" terrorists who are allied with Castro and hate the U.S.! Communist guerillas who operate in the area are eager to move-in now that the U.S. Military has gone.

Panama has signed a 50 year lease, for the two ports at each end of the Canal, with a company called "Hutchinson Wampoa" run by the right arm of China's People's Liberation Army that now controls (with priority operations) the entrance-exit ports of the Canal at the Atlantic and Pacific shores. This infringes on the passage of U.S. Warships under Panamanian Treaties.

The Panama 50 year lease gives China's Communist Party control over the most strategic waterway in the Western Hemisphere, to control facilities at both ends of the Canal and the passage of ships through the Canal. China can now assign their own pilots — according to Panama Law #5 — and can refuse access to the Canal by any ship for "business" reasons alone. Senator Trent Lott said, *"The Hutchinson Wampoa is an arm of the Peoples Liberation Army and our U.S. Naval ships will now be at the mercy of Red China."* The U.S. Navy can cut 2 full weeks off travel time to respond to crises in Europe, the Middle East, or even Cuba, by passing through the Canal.

The Canal is *vital* to American Safety yet our elected officials look the other way as China established a beachhead now within easy striking distance of cities in the U.S.A. Red Chinese J-11 Attack Jets — each of which can drop 13,000 pounds of bombs — now stand ready only 900 miles from U.S. Cities and towns.

Admiral Thomas H. Moorer, Former <u>Chairman of the Joint Chiefs of Staff</u> says, *"America is in grave danger and could face another "Pearl Harbor", — only this time it may be a <u>nuclear</u> "Pearl Harbor".*

Control of the Canal will give Red China the ability to block vital food and oil shipments to the U.S. The Canal is a vital "Choke Point" — one of 4 strategic places in the world — where a small area of land can block trade for an entire Continent. The other three "choke points" are the Suez Canal, and the two Straights near the Spratley Islands. In the past year the Clinton administration has allowed the Chinese to seize some of the Spratley Islands, — and China is currently building naval facilities there. "What are their plans" we ask?

China's take over of the Canal threatens all Americans. China is our enemy. This is the same China which stole or bought our most secret nuclear weapons and missiles and satellite technology, and tried to smuggle into California 100,000 Automatic Weapons and millions of rounds of ammunition. The same communist government that calls America their #1 Enemy and threaten to attack Los Angeles with nuclear weapons if we interfere with their planned re-conquest of Taiwan.

Through a misguided foreign policy-power that has sacrificed America's national security for **"money"** and **"personal political-power"** the Clinton/Gore administration has materially assisted Beijing's Military. Now, thanks to Bill Clinton, China is building weapons of mass destruction at breakneck speed and rapidly becoming a "global" military-power. China now has the largest military-power in the world. *Giving* control of the Canal now gives China a beachhead for expanded aggression in Latin America and a direct assault on the U.S.A. China could intimidate the *timid* U.S. into surrendering Tawian, as Panama, and who knows what else in the future, <u>without a shot being fired</u> This is "aggression" by the power of "the purse".

How much more will the U.S. allow China to control? We

are setting ourselves up for conflict! We will be forced in the not too distant future to win back militarily what we bought and built and what is rightfully ours! If we don't act *now* we will pay a high price in blood and treasure because the alternative is far worse. America has no idea of the kind of enemy whom we are dealing with here.

The Panamanian people were as surprised at this "sneaky" takeover as was the U.S.A. Over 3,000 Panamanians have lost their jobs just this past year. The people of Panama, by a three to one margin, want the U.S. to continue operating and to keep safe America's national security and treasure. China has not only taken over the Canal, but is taking over Panama itself!

According to a **"Letter to the Editor"** of the **NEW AMERICAN** magazine (Jan. 31, 2000) a Panamanian reader writes:

I just read the article entitled "Save Our Canal" by Admiral Thomas Moorer, dated August 2, 1999. In this article Admiral Moorer states, "The Chinese penetration of Panama has been primarily effected through the Panama Ports Company . . ." In my opinion, that comment should be highly publicized. There, grows a silent threat to Panama. Having lived in Panama for four years, I have seen something nobody reports as "big news": Nearly every grocery store in all of the villages I have visited throughout Panama is run by Chinese, bought with low interest loans only available to Chinese immigrants. Even those in small villages in the interior provinces such as Los Santos, which is quite far from Panama City, are owned by Chinese. According to my Panamanian friends, they charge much higher prices than the former owners who were Panamanian. I was told a typical story: A Chinese walks into a local "mini-super" and lays down an extremely large amount of cash and tells the Panamanian owner he wants to buy him out "as is" — including all stock and any outstanding debts. Almost all Panamanians I've talked to tell me that they would sell out even though a store was worth more than the money offered. If the Chinese can control the populace by denying food, staples, etc., they will have no difficulty moving in and taking over the country. I've see this happening and I predict that it will play a part in my beloved Panama's downfall. (T. Welsh, via e-mail).

The Panamanian people are strongly anti-communist. Like Americans, they knew next to nothing about this sneaky takeover of the Canal Zone and its connection with Red China and Hutchinson Wampoa, which in Panama's Law #5 (passed by Legislative Assembly in Panama in January, 1997) is called the "Panama Ports Company".

The 1977 Carter treaties were never legally ratified by Congress and are null and void; and the 1903 treaty is still in effect. The U.S. Supreme Court ruled in 1907 that the Canal Zone is indeed U.S. Territory. The Clinton administration has no legal right to give U.S. Territory away any more than they would have the right to give away North or South Carolina, to China.

The Clinton/Gore administration — in defiance of both the law and security and economic interests of the U.S.A. — went ahead with the transfer of this vital, sovereign U.S. Territory in Panama, with no regard for the legally binding Treaty of 1903.

On November 9th, 1999, Idaho Representative Helen Chenoweth-Haige introduced **House Joint Resolution HJR 77** serving notice that the 1977 Treaties are null and void and that the earlier 1903 Treaty is still in effect. We encourage people to contact their Congressmen to co-sponsor **HJR 77** and reclaim our Panama Canal. Petition papers are available for those interested to sign today.

In General Douglas MacArthur's farewell address to Congress of April 19, 1951, called *"Old Soldiers Never Die"*, he said, *"Some are blind to history's clear lessons. Appeasement begets new and bloodier wars. Like blackmail it lays the basis for new and greater demands, until, as in blackmail, 'violence' becomes the only alternative. Why surrender military advantages to an enemy in the field?"* — Asked General MacArthur.

Did we say *enemy*? Red China chose that term themselves

— that the United State is China's #1 Enemy! It is amazing that this Administration and members of Congress claim to see no evidence of a threat to our Canal in this turnover. Without a shot being fired Chinese interests have captured our most critical Seaway and supposedly ended a 400 year old dream. Can you believe it? This travesty staggers the imagination!

The construction of the Panama Canal is a tale of triumph and tragedy, the fulfillment of a 400 year old dream. The ascendancy of America to a World Power has now begun — by an illegal "Executive Order" with merely the stroke of Bill Clinton's pen.

This shows a pattern of our government in the technique of "world-merger" and the Gramcian techniques of a "patient gradualism conquest". I repeat: "This shows a pattern of our government in the technique of "world-merger" and the Gramcian techniques of a "patient gradualism conquest".

Part of the "establishment" (the "insiders") is of course the Council On Foreign Relations (CFR). Actors differ from decade to decade but their techniques are always the same. It has taken more than 50 years to bring the United Nations into focus as the world's *counterfeit* "peacekeeper". So too: the step-by step giveaway of our nation's Canal in Panama has been in the works since the Truman administration of 1945-1953.

Coast Guard Captain Russel Evens knows more about this handing over of **$32 billion dollars** of taxpayer property than any other individual on the final countdown for the Canal. (Read his book, ***"Death Knell of the Panama Canal."***) Captain Evens has spent many years studying the law involved; journeying back and forth to Panama on fact and finding missions.

The heart of this story is simple: — the transfer of the Canal is illegal and unconstitutional. Although the public has been prevented from understanding the facts, the White House and Congress are not only well aware of the giveaway, but refuse to even consider redeeming action. How has Washington been able to get away with this? The "insiders" (the "establishment") have worked long and hard with their riots, student demonstrations, Flag burnings and killings, in Panama. Truman, Eisenhower and Kennedy bowed to tiny Panama which owes its very existence to the Untied States.

By 1964 the "insiders" were ready for serious business. Lyndon Johnson was one of the early key figures in announcing "The fair claims of Panama." This is property the U.S. paid **ten million dollars in gold** for, and what is probably news to taxpayers, **an annuity — a yearly contribution — of $250,000 dollars to boot,** increased later by Eisenhower to almost **two million dollars a year!** ($1,930,000 a year)!

The Panama Canal is United States Territory —a District of the United States just like Washington, D.C.!

This surrender of U.S. Rights was approved by State Department Policy so by 1971 Secretary of State Henry Kissinger (a member of the CFR) was able to suggest to Richard Nixon (also a member of the CFR) that a termination formula be worked out, and President Nixon put Kissinger in charge. Kissinger signed a "lie" that the Canal was Panamanian Territory; not the United States Territory that it is — and the 1907 Supreme Court and U.S. Appeals Court ruled in 1972 against Kissinger's claim. Two slick operators, — who were CFR members appointed as chief negotiators and President Jimmy Carter who was also a member of CFR, — ended up with two sets or treaties not only different from each other but also violating the U.S. Constitution on the 1903 Treaty and the 1907 U.S. Supreme Court Ruling that the Canal Zone is indeed U.S. Territory (a District of the United States) — but also violated Panama's Constitution and International Law.

In 1977 after the illegal treaties, Cuba's Fidel Castro congratulated the victory. But there was and still is a fly in the ointment. The Senate refused to ratify the treaties in 1977 and in 1999. So the victory is still illegal and unconstitutional.

So on December 15, 1999, Bill Clinton by-passed congress and the senate by his "War & Emergency Powers Act" using "executive power". Where is the "right-to-know" media on this illegal giveaway of U.S. Territory in the form of dictatorship? America is a "heartbeat away" from martial law and dictatorship. This is scary? Your mighty right it is!

This "Chinagate" which is an "ongoing corruption" in America must be brought to trial if America is to remain a free nation. When foreign lobbyists with anti-American interests can walk the halls of the White House and Congress and buy our sovereignty with money, it's a sad day for America. When we see the selling of America's Soul for "money" and "power" this is TREASON! This is why we have our Constitutional Republic!

Opposition To The U.N.

"We hold these Truths to be self-evident, that all Men are created equal, that they are endowed by their Creator with certain unalienable Rights, that among these are Life, Liberty and the Pursuit of Happiness. That to secure these Rights, Governments are instituted among Men, deriving their just Powers from the Consent of the Governed. That whenever any Form of Government becomes destructive of these Ends, it is the Right of the People to alter or abolish it . . ."

The History of the United Nations is a history of repeated injuries and usurpations, all having in direct object the establishment of an absolute tyranny over the United States. To confirm this, let these facts be submitted to a candid World.

We oppose the United Nations:

1. **For imposing Taxes on us without our Consent.** Committees of the United Nations have proposed global taxes, including a Internet tax on all computer mail. Taxation without representation.

2. Because **It has affected to render the Military independent of and superior to the Civil Power.** Committees of the united Nations have proposed the establishment of a permanent standing UN army with the ability to enter any nation. Currently, soldiers of the United States, who have pledged allegiance to their native land are being forced to serve UN military missions, under foreign officers, wearing UN insignia.

3. **For depriving us, in many cases, of the benefits of trial by jury: For transporting us beyond seas to be tried for pretended offenses.** The proposed United Nations Criminal

Court will allow private citizens to be tried for violating UN treaties. No jury will be provided, no bail will be set, judges will be chosen at UN discretion even from nations hostile to the United States.

4. For taking away our Charters, abolishing our most valuable laws and altering fundamentally the forms of our governments. "Mankind's problems can no longer be solved by national governments. What is needed is a World Government": — Direct quote from the United Nation's Report on Human Development of 1994, page 88.

Clearly, the United Nations stands as a direct threat to the ideas and principles of the United States as designed and instituted by its founding Fathers.

WE, THEREFORE, the Citizens of the United States of America, assembled, appealing to the Supreme Judge of the world for the rectitude of our intentions, do, in the name, and by the authority of the good People of these United States, solemnly Publish and Declare, that these United States are, and of Right ought to be, Free and independent; that we are Absolved from all Allegiance to the United Nations organization and all political connections therewith. We therefore call upon the Congress to defend our sovereignty and Independence by enacting "The American Sovereignty Restoration Act" (H.R. 1146), which will withdraw the United States from membership in the United Nations and remove it from our shores.

Signed _____

State _____

Date _____

Words in italics are from the original Declaration of Independence.

The Main Purpose Of The 2nd Amendment

During the brief periods in world history when freedom has actually existed, freedom has usually perished because it was taken for granted. We who have tasted the fruits of freedom have customarily, in the midst of plenty, ignored the vital need to limit government. History tells us again and again that government attracts the would-be tyrant who would use government's power to enslave his fellow man.

Two of the most fundamental ingredients that shape a free society are **an armed citizenry** and **a locally controlled police** — both groups are assured by our nation's Founders in the Bill of Rights (the first 10 Amendments to our U.S. Constitution). The now beleaguered Second Amendment states very clearly that the God-given "right of the people to keep and bear arms shall not be infringed" by our government.

The main purpose of this Second Amendment has nothing to do with hunting of target shooting; it was written **to resist the aggression of tyrants** — including aggressions of our own government.

Americans anxious to preserve their liberties can gage our country's descent into a police state by pondering these questions: To what extent has "law and order" been defined as controlling people rather than protecting their rights and property? And, perhaps, most importantly, To what extent do peaceful citizens live in fear of the nation's federal police power?

In a free society we stake the future on the capacity of mankind for self-government under God; upon the capacity of each of us to govern ourselves, to sustain ourselves, and to control ourselves according to His Ten Commandments.

In a totalitarian police state, by contrast, the citizen exists to serve the state. The state can intervene at its whim into a person's private affairs; the individual is governed, controlled, and sustained by the state and state government. The state is viewed as the source of ultimate authority — not God.

When the Bureau of Alcohol, Tobacco, and Firearms (an organization for which the U.S. Constitution provides no authority whatsoever) raided Waco's Branch Davidian religious "establishment" on February 28, 1993, its stated purpose was to serve a warrant upon David Koresh for unspecified "violations" of technical weapons regulations. However, during the opening volley of the ATF raid, no one approached the door announcing the warrant, nor made even a cellular phone call to the complex.

Four ATF officers were killed in the initial exchange creating conditions for a 51 day siege that ended in the deaths of more that 80 people including woman and small children.

The government's approach to the Waco confrontation was that of the police state. The government claimed that those deaths justified the raid, in spite of the fact that the raid had CAUSED those deaths. Furthermore, during the trial of the 11 survivors, the prosecution was allowed to "examine" the religious beliefs of the Davidians as evidence of their "criminality", but — notably — spoke not a syllable about the "child abuse" allegations invoked by Attorney General Janet Reno and Mr. Clinton to justify the final assault on the Waco religious "establishment". It is apparent that Waco was a Soviet-style warning shot for devotees of politically in-correct religions.

Agents of the contemporary American state scoff at the traditional sanctity of the American home, but every dictator is sensitive to the consequences, or the possibility of arms in the hands of law abiding people.

Outside a house in Little Havana, Florida, people had been peacefully praying in preparation for the first Easter of the new millennium, when suddenly without warning, a heavily armed SWAT team authorized by Attorney General Janet Reno and Mr. Clinton burst through the door and forcefully seized little six-year old Elian Gonzales, smashed furniture, and fired tear gas into the peaceful crowds.

The Feds were not attacking a terrorist stronghold, rather unarmed Americans in the sanctity of their home. Onlookers around the world were reminded of Nazi Germany where any home could be invaded by the government at will. Janet Reno solemnly claimed that she was carrying out the law, but the Eleventh Circuit Court had sustained a decision that any individual at any age could apply for asylum, and telephone records show that his father had called his family in Miami and had asked them to take care of the young boy.

It is horrendous that the U.S. Government would resort to such heavy-handed force as was displayed on that Easter weekend. It is NOT the rule of American law when flak-jacketed heavily armed United States Marshals invade an American home in the middle of the night for any reason, however lamely justified.

In child-custody disputes, remember, the law says a family court must decide the matter. No family court had ordered Elian into his father's hands.

When Janet Reno says she's upholding the law, she is simply upholding her own position of power to subvert the Constitution of these United States, and this is a dangerous mistake.

Epilogue

America and the World stand on the brink of one of the most perilous epochs in this planet's history. The imminent danger to America and to all nations seeking peace and good will stems from the widespread acceptance of the monstrous falsehood that in order to live in a **"interdependent"** world, all nation-states must yield up their sovereignty to the United Nations cabal, resulting in:

1) A massive transfer of wealth from the taxpayers in the West to the still socialist governments of the East that remain under the control of "former" communists;

2) The gradual but accelerating merger or "convergence" of the U.S. and Russia through increasingly economic, political, social, and military agreements and arrangements;

3) The rapidly escalating transfer of power — military, regulatory, and taxing — to the United Nations.

Unless the fictional nature of these underlying developments is exposed, national suicide on a global scale will result in an all-powerful worldwide government.

The recent administration would like to make the U.N. the cornerstone of its plans to construct a New World Order.

In the early years of the Reagan Administration, U.N. bashing became positively respectable, denouncing the world body's anti-Americanism, tyranny promotion and fiscal profligacy. But the advent of Michael Gorbachev's "new thinking" in the late 1980s coincided with the beginning of a remarkable rehabilitation in the public's controlled image of the U.N. as a venue for strident anti-American diatribes, and now every day brings new appeals for the world body's intervention and so-called "expertise".

Almost one-third of Americans think the United Nations has done a good job of solving the world problems it has to face. The "rapprochement" between the former U.S.S.R. and the U.S. and the token dissolution of the Iron Curtain have been major factors contributing to the enhancement of the U.N.'s image.

Two-thirds of those surveyed thought it a good idea to build up the United Nations "emergency" force to a size great enough to deal with "brush-fires" or small wars, throughout the world while reducing the sovereignty and military strength of the U.S.A.

More than half of those questioned agree that the U.S. should abide by all World Court decisions even when they go against the American Constitution, "because this sets an example for all nations to follow".

Over one-third think that U.N. Resolutions should rule over the actions and laws of individual countries to fulfill essential U.N. functions, including ruling OVER U.S. laws even when our laws are different.

Unfortunately, like sheep being led to the slaughter, the religious media have followed right along with their secular brethren in the salvific capability of the United Nations. New Age publications virtually worship the U.N. and its cunning cohorts.

"Convergence" and "interdependence" and "harmonization" are the U.N. watchwords of the day.

Our nation is plunging headlong toward "convergence" and the intended eventual "merger". Simultaneously, our nation is being steadily drawn into the tightening noose of "interdependence". Unless this process can be stopped, it will culminate in the creation of omnipotent global governance and an "end to nationhood" — and an end to the Constitution of the United States.

U.S. Senator Jesse Helms (R-NC) warned America of "establishment insiders" who are "bringing this one world design into being, and the influence of establishment insiders over our foreign policy, if unchecked, could ultimately subvert our constitutional order." In an end-of-the century speech, Senator Helms warned that, "all of these interests are working in concert with the masters of the Kremlin in order to create what some refer to as a New World Order."

Here's what a New World Order under the United Nations would mean:

1) An end to our God-given rights guaranteed by the U.S. Constitution — freedom of religion, speech, press, and assembly, the right of trial by jury, etc.

2) National and personal disarmament, along with conscription of U.S. citizens into a United Nations One World Army or Police Force to serve the pleasures, and at the pleasure, of the U.N. hierarchy.

3) The end of private property rights and the ability to control our own homes, farms, or businesses.

4) Economic and environmental regulation at the hands of U.N. bureaucrats.

5) Loss of our Right as parents to raise and instruct our children in accordance with our personal beliefs.

6) Coercive population control measures that will determine when — or if — we may have children, and how many, — and this would include euthanasia for the aged and handicapped.

7) Unlimited global taxation.

8) A centrally managed world monetary system that will lead all but the ruling elite into poverty.

9) Environmental controls that will bring an end to the personally owned automobile and to the single family home.

10) The enthronement of an occult, New Age, New World "Religion".

11) Communist-style totalitarian dictatorship, and random, ruthless terror, torture, and extermination, to cow all peoples into abject submission to slavery.

Unfortunately — because of the great power that these Establishment Insiders wield in our major media — Senator Helm's warning never reached the American people. It was drowned under a flood of one-world propaganda on the Gorbachev "revolution" ("Perstroika") and the "new potentialities" for World Peace through a revived and strengthened United Nations.

Far from guaranteeing a new era of peace and security, the centralization of political and economic power on a planetary level can only bring about global tyranny and oppression on a scale never before imagined. The peril America and the free world face today is every bit as real though far greater in scope than what a peace-hungry world faced in 1930 prior to the Second World War.

National sovereignty is threatened as never before. As U.N. power grows, the entire world stands on the brink of **an era of totalitarian control**. We must pull back before it is too late. Simply put, unless significant numbers of Americans can be awakened from their slumbers, shaken from their apathy and ignorance, pulled away from their diversions and distractions, and convinced to work, pray, vote, speak up, struggle, and fight against the powers arrayed against them, then such a horrible fate surely awaits us all.

"The World is asleep in the cradle of infancy, dreaming away the hours."

Wake up America, and Witness to the Truth!

Made in the USA
Coppell, TX
28 September 2020

38974810R00108